TABLE OF CONTENTS

CHAPTER 1:
INTRODUCTION

Thesis

On August 9, 2010, the Secretary of Defense (SecDef) announced a number of

cost cutting recommendations designed to save $100 billion in defense spending over the

next five years, including the closure of United States Joint Forces Command

(USJFCOM) in Norfolk, Virginia. As a rationale for closing USJFCOM, the Secretary

argued that "the U.S. military has largely embraced 'jointness'[1] as a matter of culture and

practice."[2] In recommending closure, however, the Secretary seemed to suggest the

military needed to guard against a lapse or decline in the area of jointness. Perhaps

Secretary Gates understands, but does not want to admit, that cooperation between the

military Services, otherwise known broadly as jointness, is an unnatural state for the four

powerful, well-funded, and largely autonomous institutions known as the Army, Navy,

Air Force, and Marine Corps. Indeed, the Secretary's comment intimates that jointness

must be nurtured, protected, and, on occasion, enforced.

This paper disputes the Secretary's assertion that jointness has been truly

institutionalized across the Services. Moreover, it argues that the Secretary's mental

picture of the military Services as having embraced jointness is temporary and largely the

result of two activities. The first activity is USJFCOM's bridge-building between the

Services. In this capacity, the command brings commonality of policy, doctrine, joint

---

[1] Jointness refers to activities, operations, organizations, etc., in which elements of two or more Military Departments participate as per Joint Publication 1-02, Dictionary of Military and Associated Terms

[2] Robert M. Gates, "Statement on Department Efficiencies Initiative," (speech, Pentagon, Arlington, VA, August 9, 2010). In his speech, the Secretary cautioned "that we must always remain vigilant against backsliding on this [jointness] front.

training, and integration to areas where the services *should, but do not* already work well together. The second activity or function lies in the external pressure of combat, which at the tactical and operational levels removes most of the existing Service parochialism. Absent those two centripetal forces, the centrifugal forces of Service parochialism, fiscal austerity within the Department of Defense (DoD), and inter-service rivalry may extinguish any existing level of jointness and imperil the efforts of the Services to create a more effective fighting force.

Scope

The topic is especially relevant since the Unified Command Plan[3] assigns USJFCOM responsibilities as the chief advocate for jointness and enhancing levels of jointness and interoperability throughout DoD. The decision to close USJFCOM could adversely affect the entire Defense community of interest to include the Services, the Joint Staff and the combatant commands. Since the Secretary's recommendation to close USJFCOM was only recently announced, there is very little research in the subject area. The thesis will provide a unique perspective and analysis of the decision to close the command and how the decision may affect joint warfighting going forward. The thesis will study the genesis, evolution and responsibilities of USJFCOM as the joint force advocate as guided by various directives, policies, and instructions. In Chapters 1 through 3 the thesis will examine the recommendation to close USJFCOM, the process for closing a combatant command, and roles and responsibilities of the major players. Chapter 4 challenges the Secretary's recommendation to close the command and makes a case for continuing aspects of USJFCOM. Finally, in Chapters 5 and 6, the author

---

[3] 1999 *Unified Command Plan* (September 29, 1999), 7.

recommends specific USJFCOM functional mission areas that must endure in order to

posture joint forces for success in the future.

CHAPTER 2:
UNITED STATES JOINT FORCES COMMAND
HISTORY, ORGANIZATION, AND MISSION

History

In order to consider fully the topic of closure of U.S. Joint Forces Command (USJFCOM), it is important, and necessary to understand the origin and development of USJFCOM from its earliest days. USJFCOM traces its origins to the former United States Atlantic Command (USLANTCOM), making it one of the oldest unified commands within the Department of Defense.[1] USLANTCOM formally began on December 1, 1947 as a unified command when the Commander, Atlantic Fleet, was also invested with the additional duty as Commander in Chief, USLANTCOM. In those days the command was oriented on protection of the North Atlantic Ocean from a Cold War adversary, the Soviet Union. Throughout the period through the 1940s into the mid-1990s USLANTCOM was predominantly focused on a maritime mission and area of responsibility. Significant operations which the command supported in the early days included planning for the Bay of Pigs invasion of 1961; the naval quarantine of ships bound for Cuba during the Cuban missile crisis of 1962; and Operation URGENT FURY, the rescue of American medical students from the Caribbean island of Grenada, prompted by the threat of a possible communist government there.[2] In August 1985, the SecDef approved the separation of USLANTCOM from the Atlantic Fleet, as the integration of the two commands into one staff was deemed an inadequate arrangement.

The end of the Cold War lessened the importance of defending North Atlantic sea

---

[1] Leo P. Hirrel with William R. McClintock; *United States Joint Forces Command: Sixtieth Anniversary, 1947-2007* (Norfolk, VA: Office of the Command Historian, U.S. Joint Forces Command, 2007), xi.

[2] Ibid., xii-xiii.

lanes of communication, and the command concentrated on the Caribbean region and its new responsibilities for developing "joint forces." Following the passage of the Goldwater-Nichols Act in 1986, military leaders, key government officials and congressmen expressed a desire for a better process to improve interoperability among the services. Consequently, the 1993 Unified Command Plan (UCP) expanded the role of USLANTCOM to coincide with the addition of the components from all Services. In addition to its geographic responsibilities USLANTCOM received responsibility for providing conventional joint forces within the continental United States (CONUS) to combatant commanders across the globe. The new UCP also assigned USLANTCOM responsibility for providing joint training to its component forces.[3] In a separate document, the "Forces for Memorandum," the Service component commands -- Marine Forces Atlantic, Atlantic Fleet, the Army's Forces Command, and the Air Force's Air Combat Command -- were subordinated to USLANTCOM. This marked the first time that USLANTCOM had permanent, peacetime command of elements of all four services. Finally, on 1 October 1999, USLANTCOM was redesignated as the USJFCOM.

Organization

The organization of USJFCOM is very similar to the general staff structure introduced by the French during the 19th century. There are eight directorates, J1 through J9, which handle responsibilities from Personnel (J1) through Joint Concept Development and Experimentation (J9). The majority of directorates are headed by flag or general officers, or Senior Executive Service civilians. In executing its day-to-day responsibilities, USJFCOM is guided by a weighty number of directives, instructions and

---

[3] Hirrel with McClintock, xiii.

5

memoranda from the Secretary of Defense (SecDef), and the Chairman of the Joint

Chiefs of Staff (CJCS), as well as the UCP signed by the President of the United States.

The best approach to acquaint the reader with the enormity of USJFCOM's

responsibilities is to summarize its major UCP mission areas as well as describe its

subordinate commands and activities.

The USJFCOM organization is depicted in the following illustration:

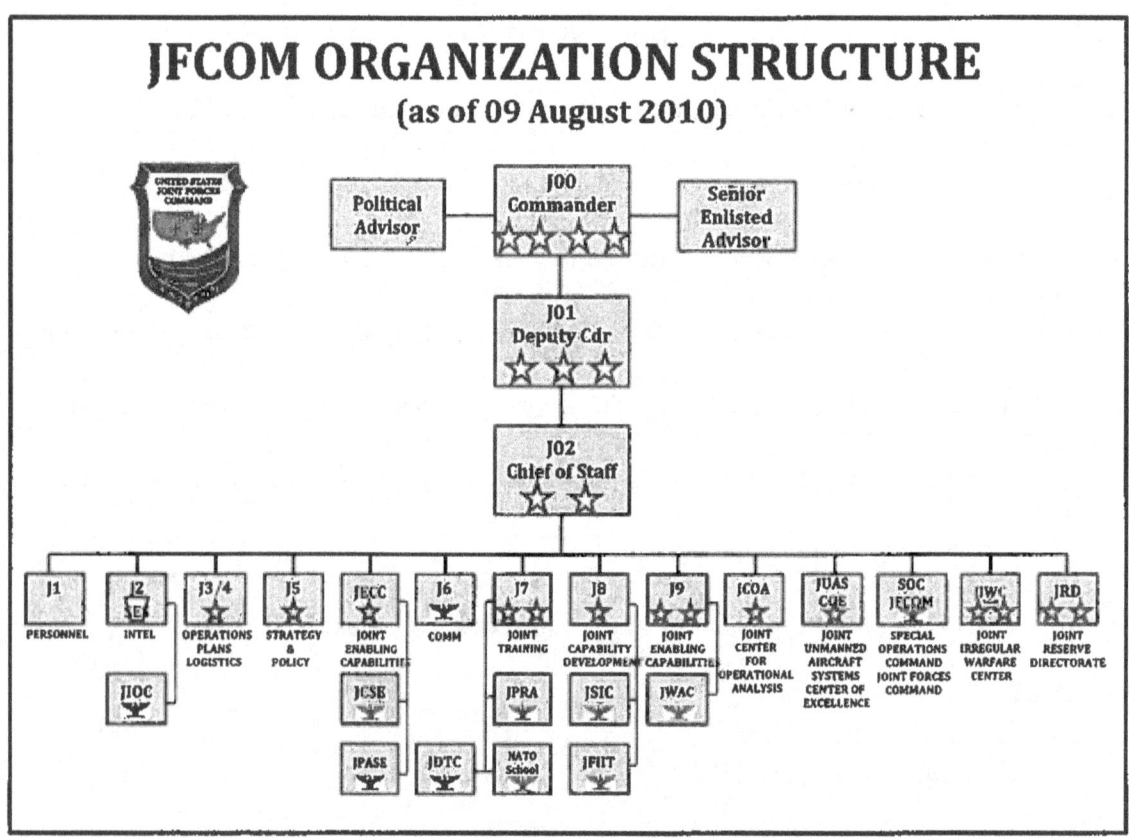

**Figure II-1: USJFCOM Staff and Subordinate Commands and Activities
(Source: USJFCOM Command Brief dated 06 August 2010)**

Unified Command Plan Responsibilities

Although the 1999 UCP was effective on 1 October 1999, the ceremony officially

changing the command's name to U.S. Joint Forces Command occurred on 7 October

1999.[4] To the casual observer very little change was apparent, but in the words of the first USJFCOM Commander, Admiral Harold W. Gehman, the name change was "subtle but very profound." The new name signaled that henceforth USJFCOM would be expected to lead the U.S. military in enhancing joint force interoperability.[5] In the twelve years since the name change, the USJFCOM mission grew exponentially. In 2010, the USJFCOM mission was to provide mission-ready, joint capable forces and support the development and integration of joint, interagency, and multinational capabilities to meet the present and future operational needs of the Joint Force.[6] The mission has three distinct elements: providing joint capable forces, developing and integrating joint capabilities, and determining future requirements to support the joint force.

Since USJFCOM's designation as an advocate for the joint force, each subsequent iteration of the UCP (1999, 2002, 2004, 2006 and 2008) further defined and expanded the command's portfolio of specific tasks. The 2008 UCP, the most current, assigns USJFCOM six functional responsibilities intended to transform U.S. military forces to meet the security challenges of the 21st century.[7] The mission areas include Joint Force Provider, Joint Force Integrator, Joint Concept Development and Experimentation, Joint Force Trainer, Joint Force Enabler, and Joint Task Force Headquarters Standards Development. Each of the mission areas will be discussed below.

---

[4] Hirrel with McClintock, 53.

[5] Ibid., 53.

[6] U.S. Joint Forces Command, Command Overview Briefing, Norfolk, VA: Office of Public Affairs, U.S. Joint Forces Command, August 6, 2010, slide 2.

[7] 2008 *Unified Command Plan* (December 17, 2008), 21.

Joint Force Provider

Initially assigned to USLANTCOM in October 1993, the current UCP assigns the joint force provider mission to USJFCOM charging them with deploying trained and ready joint forces and informed military force options to satisfy combatant command requirements. As the DoD joint force provider, USJFCOM's Operations, Plans, Logistics and Engineering Directorate (J3/J4) assigns trained and capable conventional forces based in CONUS to combatant commanders in the field. Building the joint force requires a considerable degree of coordination with active, National Guard and Reserve elements of the armed forces to ensure the deployment of an integrated, task-organized team. Nearly 50% of all active duty forces are assigned to USJFCOM with visibility through its subordinate Service components of approximately 80% (1.1 million personnel) of all forces including Guard and Reserve components. As a concurrent responsibility, USJFCOM also serves as the DoD Joint Deployment Process Owner with responsibilities for maintaining the global capacity for military force power projection and redeployment.[8] As an example, in 2006, USJFCOM developed recommendations and coordinated the deployment of more than 290,000 personnel, including individual augments, in support of validated combatant command requirements.[9]

Joint Force Trainer

Although UCP 2008 directs each combatant command to be prepared to provide trained and ready joint forces to other combatant commands, it charges USJFCOM to lead joint force training under the cognizance of the C JCS. This responsibility also

---

[8] 2008 *Unified Command Plan* (December 17, 2008), 22.

[9] U.S. Joint Forces Command, "USJFCOM as Force Provider," http://www.jfcom.mil/about/forceprov.html (accessed October 29, 2010).

traces its roots to October 1993 when, then USLANTCOM, was given the mission to conduct joint training of CONUS-based forces. The Joint Training Directorate/Joint Warfighting Center (J7) trains forces, develops doctrine, leads training requirements analysis and provides a globally distributed and interoperable training environment to improve joint force readiness.[10] As coordinator of the military's overall joint training effort, the J7 conducts joint exercises, facilitating the development and execution of rigorous and realistic collective joint training. Additionally, it aids the Service training programs by providing joint context and capabilities, and its mission rehearsal exercise program prepares combined and joint staffs for contingency operations. As the major production center for joint doctrine assessment and development, USJFCOM aids in the development of handbooks, newsletters and white papers about new or emerging operational issues. Finally, the USJFCOM J7 develops and delivers joint professional military education for senior military leadership in complex environments through the Capstone, Keystone and Pinnacle courses. Individual joint training is also provided for about 100,000 registered users of Joint Knowledge Online, an advanced distributed online learning network that provides immediate access to joint knowledge resources.[11]

Joint Concept Development and Experimentation

UCP 1999 included a provision for specifying USJFCOM as the executive agent[12] for joint experimentation. In UCP 2004, that responsibility was expanded to give

---

[10] U.S. Joint Forces Command, "Joint Training Directorate/Joint Warfighting Center (J7)," http://www.jfcom.mil/about/abt_j7.htm (accessed November 03, 2010).

[11] Ibid.

[12] As per Joint Publication 1-02, *Dictionary of Military and Associated Terms*, executive agent (EA) is a term used to indicate a delegation of authority by the Secretary of Defense to a subordinate to act on behalf of the Secretary of Defense. Designation as executive agent, in and of itself, confers no authority. The exact nature and scope of the authority delegated must be stated in the document designating the executive agent. An executive agent may be limited to providing only administration and support or coordinating common

USJFCOM responsibility for coordinating all concept development and experimentation efforts of other services and combatant command. Today, the Joint Concept Development and Experimentation Directorate/Joint Futures Laboratory (J9) integrates multinational and interagency warfighting transformation and experimentation efforts to support joint interoperability and develop future joint warfighting capabilities.[13] Operationally relevant solutions are rapidly delivered to support current operations and drive changes to doctrine, organization, training, materiel, leadership, personnel and facilities and policy to better enable the future joint force.[14]

Joint Force Integrator

In January 1998, USJFCOM was assigned as the Joint Force Integrator, to develop joint, combined, interagency capabilities to improve interoperability and enhancing capabilities of technology, systems, and doctrine. In coordination with the CJCS, USJFCOM's Joint Capability Development Directorate (J8) leads development of joint concepts, requirements and integrated architectures for joint command and control to ensure integration and interoperability from the tactical to the strategic level.[15] The joint integration mission area also encompasses the Chairman's joint doctrine program to develop and maintain joint doctrine publications.

---

functions or it may be delegated authority, direction, and control over specified resources for specified purposes.

[13] 2008 *Unified Command Plan* (December 17, 2008), 22.

[14] U.S. Joint Forces Command, "Joint Concept Development and Experimentation Directorate (J9)," http://www.jfcom.mil/about/abt_j9.htm (accessed November 03, 2010).

[15] 2008 *Unified Command Plan* (December 17, 2008), 22.

Joint Force Enabler

To streamline the rapid formation and organization of joint task force headquarters, USJFCOM's subordinate Joint Enabling Capabilities Command (JECC) is responsible for providing forces that can rapidly deploy critical command and control capabilities to support newly-established joint force headquarters. The JECC maintains two core elements capable of short notice deployments. These core elements are augmented with deployable communications assets from the Joint Communications Support Element, intelligence personnel, public affairs and personnel recovery expertise. Although each geographic combatant command is directed to establish and maintain a standing joint force headquarters (SJFHQ) element, UCP 2008 directs USJFCOM to establish and maintain two SJFHQ elements. These USJFCOM JECC elements train continuously with operational joint forces from other combatant commands in order to enhance readiness for operational-level joint command and control.

Joint Task Force Headquarters Standards Development

The last major mission area was assigned to USJFCOM by UCP 2008. USJFCOM was tasked to recommend to the CJCS a set of standard tasks and conditions that could be used to certify the readiness of designated JTF headquarters. These standards guide the combatant commands as they certify joint task force headquarters from within their subordinate elements.

Subordinate Commands and Activities

In addition to the general staff structure, USJFCOM also has a number of subordinate commands and activities as depicted in Figure II-1. The first of these subordinate commands or activities was assigned as a result of the Quadrennial Defense

Review (QDR) of 1997 and Defense Reform Initiative of 1997. On 1 October 1998, five formerly CJCS-controlled activities were resubordinated under the command and control of USJFCOM. All were performing valid functions; however, those activities were providing support at the operational and tactical levels which allowed the Joint Staff to maintain its focus at the strategic level.[16] A brief description of the thirteen subordinate commands and activities follows.

Joint Communications Support Element (JCSE)

The JCSE mission is to provide tactical communications equipment and support services tailored to the needs of a joint task force headquarters. The JCSE has the ability to bridge the communications and interoperability problems between services, coalitions and host nation partners.[17] The unit is comprised of active duty, Guard, and Reserve forces based at MacDill Air Force Base, Tampa, Florida. This joint unit deploys globally within hours of notification to provide command, control, communications and computers (C4) support to combatant commands including United States Special Operations Command (USSOCOM).

Joint Public Affairs Support Element (JPASE)

The JPASE was formed to provide trained, equipped, scalable and expeditionary joint public affairs (JPA) capability to support world-wide operational requirements. JPASE provides the supported joint force commander (JFC) with an early entry capability to enable the JFC to gain and maintain the initiative in the information

---

[16] William S. Cohen, Defense Reform Initiative Report, Washington, DC: Office of the Secretary of Defense, November 1997, Appendix C-7.

[17] U.S. Joint Forces Command, "Joint Communications Support Element (JCSE)," http://www.jfcom.mil/about/com_jcse.htm (accessed October 22, 2010).

domain.[18] Based in Suffolk, Virginia, the JPASE supports three main mission areas including support to joint training and exercise, joint proponency for public affairs concerns, and providing ready-deployable, joint public affairs teams in support of operational requirements.

Joint Deployment Training Center (JDTC)

The mission of the JDTC is to provide training to personnel from combatant commands, the Services, DoD, other agencies and professional military education institutions on tools such as the Global Command and Control System-Joint (GCCS-J) and global force management applications for planning and executing command and control of deployment and combat operations, joint logistics and force management. This training supports overseas contingencies, crisis actions and humanitarian operations.[19] Based at Joint Base Langley-Fort Eustis, Virginia, the center provides in-resident, mobile training team, and distributed learning support.

Joint Personnel Recovery Agency (JPRA)

The Commander, USJFCOM is designated as the DoD Executive Agent for personnel recovery (PR) and coordinates and advances joint personnel recovery capabilities. USJFCOM has designated its subordinate activity, JPRA, as the office of primary responsibility for DoD-wide personnel recovery matters, executing the day-to-day responsibilities of executive agent. JPRA enables commanders, individuals, recovery forces and supporting organizations to execute their personnel recovery responsibilities

---

[18] U.S. Joint Forces Command, "Joint Public Affairs Support Element (JPASE)," http://www.jfcom.mil/about/com_jpase.htm (accessed October 22, 2010).

[19] U.S. Joint Forces Command, "Joint Deployment Training Center (JDTC)," http://www.jfcom.mil/about/com_jdtc.htm (accessed on October 22, 2010).

and to accomplish the five PR tasks of report, locate, support, recover and reintegrate.[20]

JPRA, created in 1999, is located at Fort Belvoir, Virginia, and is a subordinate activity

of USJFCOM's Joint Training Directorate (J7)/Joint Warfighting Center (JWFC).

Joint Systems Integration Center (JSIC)

The JSIC brings together operational and technical expertise, technology, state-of-

the-art facilities, defendable and repeatable scientific methodology and extensive joint

command and control (C2) capabilities to identify and solve joint and coalition

interoperability problems.[21] Since its subordination to USJFCOM in 1998, the JSIC's

main mission is to assess, investigate, isolate and document systems interoperability

issues and recommend needed improvements. Based in Suffolk, Virginia, the JSIC

supports interoperability demonstrations, capability integration, capability assessments

and support to the C2 capability portfolio manager.

Joint Fires Integration and Interoperability Team (JFIIT)

JFIIT is chartered with improving the integration, interoperability, and

effectiveness of joint fires at the tactical level. Established in February 2005, the team

provides assistance to JFCs and Service headquarters in the planning, coordination, and

execution of joint fires at the tactical level. Based at Eglin AFB, FL, JFIIT improves joint

fires by providing solutions that produce effective target acquisition, command and

control (C2), and interoperable firing systems, thereby reducing fratricide and collateral

damage.[22]

---

[20] U.S. Joint Forces Command, "Joint Personnel Recovery Agency (JPRA)," http://www.jfcom.mil/about/com_jpra.htm (accessed on October 22, 2010).

[21] U.S. Joint Forces Command, "Joint Systems Integration Center (JSIC)," http://www.jfcom.mil/about/com_jsic.htm (accessed October 22, 2010).

[22] U.S. Joint Forces Command, "Joint Fires Integration and Interoperability Team (JFIIT)," http://www.jfcom.mil/about/com_jfiit.htm (accessed October 22, 2010).

Joint Warfare Analysis Center (JWAC)

JWAC provides combatant commands, Joint Staff, and other customers with precise technical solutions in order to carry out the national security and military strategies of the United States. JWAC's comprehensive technical analysis informs and supports decision-makers both in combat and in policy-making sessions at the highest levels of government. JWAC is uniquely positioned to flexibly solve a broad range of problems, examine intractable issues from an unfettered viewpoint, and provide commanders with full spectrum engagement options encompassing all elements of national power.[23] JWAC is located on the Naval Support Facility in Dahlgren, Virginia.

Joint Intelligence Operations Center (JIOC)

The Intelligence Directorate (J2) JIOC develops, integrates, trains and provides joint intelligence capabilities to meet present and future needs of joint forces.[24] These efforts align with USJFCOM's major mission areas and include joint intelligence training and education, intelligence force provision, intelligence capability development and intelligence concept development and experimentation. The JIOC is located on the Naval Support Activity, Norfolk, Virginia.

Joint Enabling Capabilities Command (JECC)

The mission of the JECC is to provide unique, mission-ready support to JFCs to aid the accelerated establishment and increased effectiveness of their headquarters and the ability to control the integrated employment of air, land, maritime and information

---

[23] U.S. Joint Forces Command, "Joint Warfare Analysis Center (JWAC)," http://www.jfcom.mil/about/com_jwac.htm (accessed October 22, 2010).

[24] U.S. Joint Forces Command, "Intelligence Directorate (J2), Joint Intelligence Operations Center (JIOC)," http://www.jfcom.mil/about/abt_j2.htm (accessed October 22, 2010).

capabilities in pursuit of operational level campaign objectives.[25] The JECC deploys teams to assist JTF commanders with capabilities in four critical areas - Operations, Plans, Information Superiority and Knowledge Management, and Logistics. These capabilities satisfy USJFCOM responsibilities specified in the CJCS Global Response Force execute order.

Joint Center for Operational Analyses (JCOA)

JCOA is the subordinate activity that collects, analyzes and disseminates lessons learned and best practices in order to integrate recommendations and improve the joint force warfighting capability across the full spectrum of military operations. Based in Suffolk, Virginia, JCOA was created in 2003 to study the performance of the joint force during the invasion of Iraq in Operation IRAQI FREEDOM. Since then, JCOA has expanded its research to support joint operations around the world, covering issues including humanitarian assistance and disaster relief operations, civil-military coordination efforts, the effectiveness of information activities, and mitigating the effects of civilian casualties in counterinsurgency operations.[26] The focus of JCOA analysis has been joint issues at the operational level of war. The studies are conducted at joint headquarters worldwide, providing analysis directly to the senior leadership of the supported command. JCOA disseminates the results of its findings through briefs, reports, papers, journals and other products which are shared directly with DoD, interagency and multinational partners.

---

[25] U.S. Joint Forces Command, "Joint Enabling Capability Command (JECC)," http://www.jfcom.mil/about/fact_jec.html; (accessed October 22, 2010).

[26] U.S. Joint Forces Command, "Joint Center for Operational Analysis (JCOA)," http://www.jfcom.mil/about/fact_jcoa.html (accessed October 26, 2010).

Joint Unmanned Aircraft Systems--Center of Excellence (JUAS--COE)

Headquartered at Creech AFB, Nevada, the JUAS--COE focuses on joint

unmanned aircraft systems (UAS) employment and training standards.[27] Its customers

include the joint operator, Services and combatant commands. JUAS--COE project

teams work to optimize training and employment related to UAS collection, exploitation

and dissemination and improve measures of effectiveness for full motion video support to

command and control (C2), intelligence, surveillance and reconnaissance (ISR), and

force application mission areas. JUAS--COE leverages existing combatant command and

Service initiatives and activities to provide joint integrated solutions and improved

interoperability.

Special Operations Command, USJFCOM (SOCJFCOM)

SOCJFCOM is a subordinate command of USJFCOM and is the primary joint

special operations forces (SOF) trainer and integrator within DoD. SOCJFCOM's

mission is to train conventional and special operations joint force commanders and their

staffs in the employment of SOF, focusing on the full integration of SOF and

conventional forces in both planning and execution to enhance warfighting readiness.[28]

Located in Suffolk, VA, SOCJFCOM has responsibilities to support Title 10 missions for

both USJFCOM and USSOCOM, which positions them to support SOF-conventional

force training and integration.

Joint Irregular Warfare Center (JIWC)

The mission of the JIWC is to proactively coordinate, prioritize, and provide

---

[27] U.S. Joint Forces Command, "Joint Unmanned Aircraft Systems-Center of Excellence (JUAS--COE)," http://www.jfcom.mil/about/com_juas.html (accessed October 26, 2010)).

[28] U.S. Joint Forces Command, "Special Operations Command (SOCJFCOM)," http://www.jfcom.mil/about/com_socjfcom.html (accessed October 26, 2010).

subject matter expertise on all irregular warfare (IW) matters. Recognizing the emphasis placed on IW in the 2006 QDR and 2008 National Defense Strategy (NDS), USJFCOM established the center in 2008 to institutionalize IW as a general purpose force core competency today and in the future. Headquartered in Suffolk, Virginia, the JIWC integrates IW activities across USJFCOM directorates, the DoD, multinational and interagency partners. The JIWC ensures joint IW capabilities meet combatant commander campaign and complex contingency requirements for joint IW concept development and experimentation, training, doctrine and capability development.[29] Additionally, the JIWC executes USJFCOM's responsibilities as the DoD executive agent for joint urban operations..

Summary

USJFCOM responsibilities involve the command in both current and future operations. To enable "readiness today" the command is focused on joint force training, joint force providing and joint force enabling missions. The joint concept development and experimentation and joint force integration mission areas provide a framework for how the joint force will operate in the future with joint and interoperable systems and capabilities. When considering the scope and scale of USJFCOM's immense undertakings and the influence and ramifications across the Services, interagency and DoD communities, the SecDef recommendation to close the command threatens to derail the sole advocate for joint forces. In the years since 1998, the landscape of USJFCOM's subordinate commands and activities has changed based on departmental reviews and UCP changes, and as of October 2010 there were at least thirteen subordinate commands

---

[29] U.S. Joint Forces Command, "Joint Irregular Warfare Center (JIWC)," http://www.jfcom.mil/about/abt_jiwc.html (accessed October 26, 2010).

or activities depicted in the organization chart. The frequent and continued assignment of seemingly disparate responsibilities to USJFCOM has diluted the command's focus of effort and increased the number of personnel assigned. Moreover, the burgeoning size of the USJFCOM headquarters placed them in the crosshairs of the DoD Efficiencies Task Force as a leading candidate for downsizing and budgetary reforms. The transfer to USJFCOM of an ever increasing number of dissimilar responsibilities and subordinate activities calls to mind the Mr. Potato Head[30] toy in which children manufacture a face by attaching different plastic parts, e.g., ears, nose, eyes, etc., to a plastic model.

In the next chapter, the recommendation to close USJFCOM will be addressed. In doing so, the paper will consider whether the mission has been accomplished, examine potential effects of closure, and explore the process for closing a combatant command.

---

[30] Mr. Potato Head is an American toy consisting of a plastic model of a potato which can be decorated with a variety of attachable plastic parts such as ears and eyes to make a face. The toy was first manufactured and distributed by Hasbro in 1952, as per the *Museum of Childhood* website http://www.vam.ac.uk/moc/collections/toys/construction_toys/mr_potato_head/index.html (accessed November 03, 2010).

CHAPTER 3:
CLOSING USJFCOM

The previous chapter described the evolution of USJFCOM as a combatant command, and the transfer of responsibilities to them as prescribed in the various Unified Command Plan (UCP) documents. It also summarized the myriad of subordinate commands and activities subordinated to USJFCOM beginning with the recommendations of the Defense Review Initiative Report of 1997. This chapter will examine the Secretary of Defense (SecDef) recommendation to close USJFCOM, the UCP process, and the roles of decision-makers involved in the process of closing a combatant command.

Defense Business Board Recommendation

The first indication that USJFCOM was targeted for closure surfaced during a July 22, 2010 presentation by the Defense Business Board (DBB). In May 2010, the SecDef tasked the DBB to form a task group to study and make recommendations on options to materially reduce Department of Defense (DoD) overhead and increase the efficiency of DoD business operations.[1] During the public session of the July 2010 DBB quarterly meeting, Mr. Arnold Punaro delivered a briefing entitled "Reducing Overhead and Improving Business Operations." The task group briefing highlighted a number of observations regarding DoD overhead and expenditures which threaten national security from the department's fiscal posture. The DBB analysis concluded that DoD total budget authority spending had increased almost 44% during the period 1980 to 2010, while the number of military personnel shrank 29%, the number of Navy ships decreased 47%, the

---

[1] Arnold Punaro, "Reducing Overhead and Improving Business Operations," Defense Business Board Briefing, Public Session, July 22, 2010.

number of active Army divisions declined 49%, and the total active inventory of Air Force fighter/attack aircraft was reduced 54%.[2] A comparison of prior administration defense budgets indicated that although defense spending had increased in constant or inflated dollars, the budget no longer purchased as much; in some cases outputs were down nearly 50%. DoD buying power had eroded and the American taxpayer was paying "more for less." In short, overhead costs were preventing DoD from obtaining the maximum combat power for the resources spent.

The DBB presentation also addressed a number of opportunities for short- and long-term budget savings that included both process and organizational change recommendations. Among those business practices recommended for immediate consideration was a recommendation to downsize combatant commands, beginning with the elimination of USJFCOM. In discussing the size of the combatant command staffs and budgets, the briefing singled out USJFCOM as the largest staff of the ten combatant commands and employing more contractors than military personnel and government civilians combined.[3] As of July 2009, the number of government (military and civilian) personnel was approximately 3,000 and the number of contractors was depicted as approximately 3,300 personnel.[4] An additional criticism was the number of joint activities and subordinate commands at USJFCOM.[5] Figure III-1 is a slide from the DBB briefing that represents personnel manning at all ten combatant commands.

---

[2] Punaro, "Reducing Overhead and Improving Business Operations," slide 8.

[3] Ibid., slide 30.

[4] Author's note: Reports on number of government and contractor personnel assigned to JFCOM vary. JFCOM self-reported 1561 military, 1596 civilian and 2565 full-time, contractor personnel as of August 13, 2010.

[5] Punaro, slide 31.

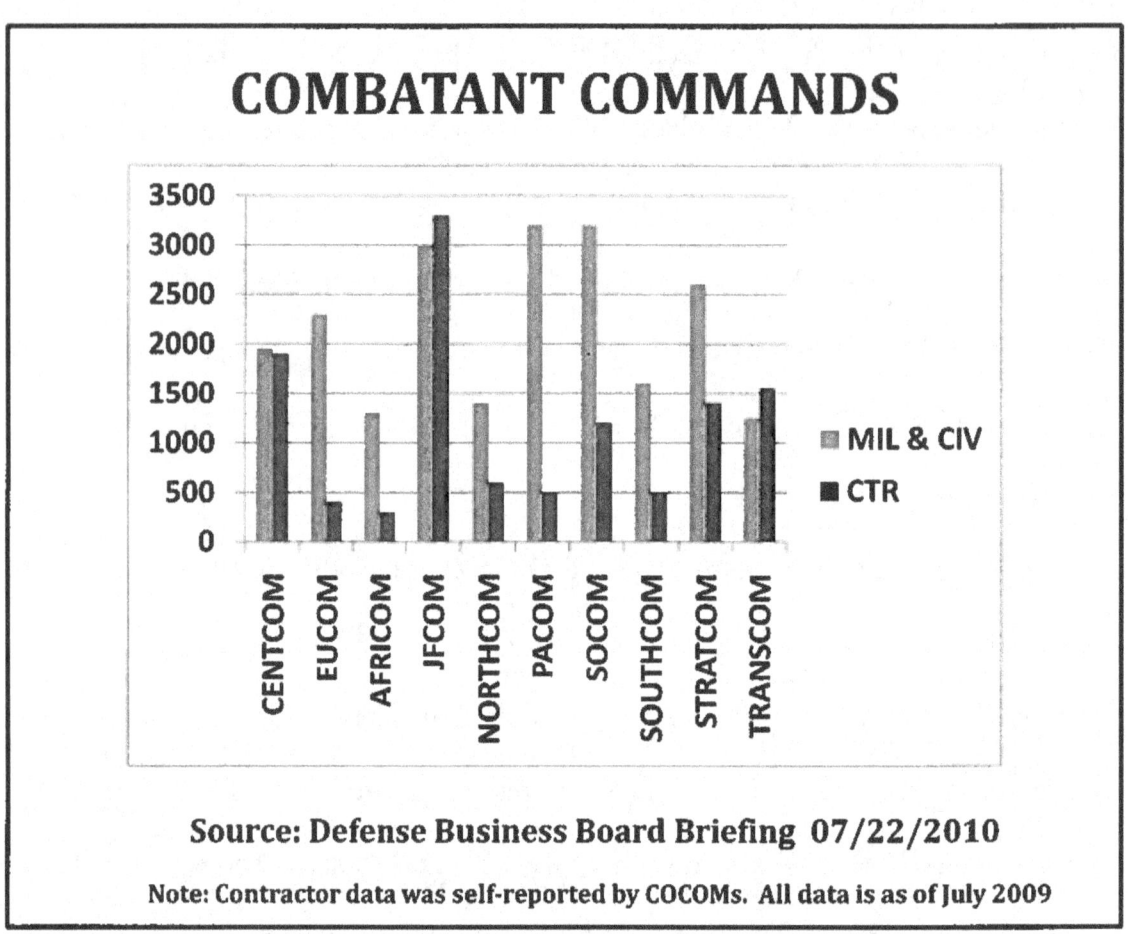

COMBATANT COMMANDS

Source: Defense Business Board Briefing 07/22/2010

Note: Contractor data was self-reported by COCOMs. All data is as of July 2009

Figure III-1: Combatant Command Manning

Although the DBB recommended eliminating USJFCOM, their report did not address mitigation of the risks that would result from closing the command. One might take the position that risk mitigation was not included in their original tasking, however, a failure to consider the risks of their recommendations detracts from, or calls into question, their otherwise detailed investigation and analysis. In researching this paper, the author determined that the DBB completed its study without having made a visit to USJFCOM. Additionally, based on a review of the DBB briefing, the sole criteria for recommending closure of USJFCOM appears to be quantitative–the numbers of personnel assigned and the number of joint commands and activities subordinated to USJFCOM–rather than a qualitative analysis of what value USJFCOM adds to joint warfighting. A thorough review of the DBB website and an e-mail request for the final DBB task force study failed to produce any detailed data that supports the DBB recommendation or any analysis of alternatives considered in formulating the recommendation. Moreover, a House Armed Services Committee (HASC) letter to the SecDef requesting business case analysis data prepared by DoD or the DBB documenting savings and reductions in overhead within the defense enterprise resultant from USJFCOM's closure[6] went unanswered.

It's all about the *Benjamins*

Following closely on the heels of the DBB briefing, the SecDef delivered a speech on August 9, 2010 entitled "Statement of Department Efficiencies Initiatives" that announced major changes in the defense budget were necessary to sustain the force structure and strengthen modernization programs. The Secretary drew attention to the difficult economic and fiscal situation facing the nation and outlined a number of measures to be adopted to reduce overhead and eliminate excess spending. Secretary Gates described eight specific initiatives that would result in a more efficient and effective way of doing business; one of those initiatives contained a recommendation to close USJFCOM.[7] In analyzing the DBB recommendation and the Secretary's speech on DoD efficiencies, it is apparent that the rationale for closing USJFCOM is purely financial. The SecDef wanted $100 billion of overhead savings over a five-year period and any savings from a reduction in overhead costs would be directed towards force

---

[6] J. Randy Forbes, Howard P. McKeon, and Robert J. Wittman, House Committee on Armed Forces to Secretary of Defense, August 31, 2010.

[7] Robert M. Gates, "Statement on Department Efficiencies Initiative" (speech, Pentagon, Arlington, VA, August 9, 2010).

structure and modernization. The Secretary's stated goal was for the top line budget expenditure to remain constant and all savings directed to where they were needed.

Although Secretary Gates' described USJFCOM as having fulfilled its established purpose by instilling jointness across the military as evidenced by nearly two decades of operational experience, he left open the possibility that the command might not be closing completely when he acknowledged that USJFCOM's missions would be evaluated for retention and reassignment to another organization. Secretary Gates' announced timeline for closure of USJFCOM and other organizations recommended for closure or consolidation would occur within the next six-to-twelve months. Conversely, it took nearly five months for the SecDef to provide any of the specific details of the defense efficiencies announced in August 2010. During a news conference on January 6, 2011, Secretary Gates expanded on his August 2010 recommendation and announced $154 billion in defense efficiencies over the five years ending in 2016 with approximately $70 billion of that sum to be reinvested in high priority military programs and capabilities. Regarding USJFCOM, the Secretary reported approximately 50% of the capabilities would be eliminated or disestablished. Although the refinement of the details was still underway, 50% of USJFCOM's capabilities would be retained under other organizations in the Norfolk/Suffolk, Virginia area.[8] The retention of 50% of USJFCOM capabilities is consistent with statements made by the command's leadership that advised a significant reshaping of the command would occur.[9]

---

[8] Robert M. Gates, "Statement on Department Budget and Efficiencies" (Arlington, VA: Dept of Defense, January 6, 2011).

[9] Raymond T. Odierno, "CDR, U.S. Joint Forces Command announcement November 22, 2010," U.S. Joint forces Command, https://us.jfcom.mil/sites/JTPT/Pages/Default.aspx (accessed January 5, 2011).

Although Secretary Gates' August 2010 announcement recommended the closure of USJFCOM, Presidential endorsement or approval of the endorsement did not occur until January 6, 2011. In the intervening five months since the August 2010 recommendation, the Joint Staff and DoD Efficiencies Task Forces collected data on USJFCOM mission areas and responsibilities to analyze and develop an implementation plan for approval of the closure by the President. The rough outline of the plan was to be announced at a future date. In reflecting on the delay in releasing the implementation plan to close USJFCOM, a number of possible factors affecting the decision spring to mind:

- The Secretary's recommendation to close USJFCOM was based only on a cursory analysis and more time was needed to study the decision to identify the merits of closing the command and develop an implementation plan.

- The decision affects potentially 5,700 employees and their family members, and the DoD is proceeding with deliberation to minimize personnel turbulence.

- Presidential approval of the decision to close USJFCOM may have been delayed until after the mid-term election held in November 2010. Governor McDonnell and members of the Virginia congressional delegation have been vocal critics of the SecrDef's recommendation and have sought, with only limited success, detailed analysis, projected cost savings and justification for closing USJFCOM.

- A decision to close a combatant command is of such magnitude that a deliberative process and approach are mandated.

The Unified Command Plan and the Process for Closing a Combatant Command

The Process for Closing a Combatant Command

The process for closing a combatant command is a highly contentious issue involving a number of parties and consideration of a number of factors. The UCP is the document that describes the state of the joint command structure within DoD. The UCP is an executive document signed by the President. The purpose of the UCP is to provide effective control of U.S. forces in peace and war. The UCP delineates a command structure from the President thru the SecDef to the combatant command level. It establishes unified and specified commands and assigns missions and functions to those commands.[10]

Although there is no prescribed process for affecting changes to the UCP, Title 10 U.S.C. § 118 directs the SecDef to comment on the advisability of revisions to the UCP as a result of the National Defense Strategy (NDS) in his report to Congress on the quadrennial defense review (QDR).[11] The principal players involved in a decision to close a combatant command include the President of the United States, the SecDef, the CJCS, and Congress. In most instances changes to the UCP are recommended by the CJCS. These changes traditionally address military concerns about changing threats, organization or force structure. All recommended changes to the UCP must be reviewed by the SecDef. Occasionally, Congress has taken legislative action that has directly

---

[10] William C. Story, *Military Changes to the Unified Command Plan: Background and Issues for Congress,* (Washington, DC: Congressional Research Service, Library of Congress, June 21, 1999), CRS-2.

[11] *Quadrennial Defense Review*, 10 U.S.C. 118, February 1, 2010 http://uscode.house.gov (accessed March 28, 2011).

resulted in modifications to the UCP to accommodate certain interests and concerns.[12]

This section will address the roles and responsibilities of the actors mentioned above, and

outline what has transpired since the SecDef's recommendation to close the USJFCOM.

President of the United States

As the Commander-in-Chief of the Armed Forces, the President of the United

States influences the combatant command structure in a number of ways. The President,

through the SecDef with the advice and assistance of the CJCS, establishes combatant

commands for the performance of military missions and prescribes the force structure of

the commands.[13] There are two primary executive-level documents approved by the

President that are germane: the UCP and the National Security Strategy (NSS). The

UCP provides basic guidance to all combatant commanders by specifying combatant

command missions and tasks, combatant command force structure, and delineating

geographic areas of responsibility. The current UCP was published on December 17,

2008. The NSS is an executive document that is prepared for Congress which outlines

the national security issues and the administration's approach in confronting those issues.

The Goldwater-Nichols Act of 1986 provides the legal precedent for the NSS. The most

recent NSS was published in May 2010.

Secretary of Defense

The SecDef is the civilian head of the DoD and the principal defense advisor to

the President of the United States. The DoD Reorganization Act of 1958 signed by

President Eisenhower established a clear line of command from the President through the

---

[12] Story, *Military Changes to the Unified Command Plan: Background and Issues for Congress,* CRS-1.

[13] U.S. Joint Chiefs of Staff, *Unified Action Armed Forces (UNAAF),* JCS Pub 0-2, (Washington DC: 02 May 2007, w/ change 1 of 20 March 2009), xiii.

SecDef with the Joint Chiefs of Staff (JCS) acting as the Secretary's staff to the unified and specified commands.[14] The Secretary exercises his influence on the UCP through issuance of the NDS. The NDS provides guidance on how the DoD will support the President's NSS and also informs the National Military Strategy (NMS) and other relevant strategy documents. The NDS is issued periodically; the current NDS was published in February 2011. The NDS along with the Guidance for Employment of the Force (GEF) provides the Secretary's direction to the Armed Forces on "what" missions they will accomplish. Mission tasking then drives force structure and organizations.

Chairman of the Joint Chiefs of Staff (CJCS)

Much of the history of the UCP involves debate over how combatant commands should be organized. These disputes usually centered on whether to arrange the commands around geographic areas as opposed to functional groupings of forces. In the early years, Service choices were often a deciding factor in resolving the disputes.[15] As a result of the National Security Act of 1947, the JCS was established and the terms of the UCP became more joint and less focused on traditional Service prerogatives. Prior to the Goldwater-Nichols Act of 1986, the JCS made only marginal changes to the UCP, and Congress and the President had to prompt significant change. The Chairman's role was further strengthened with the passage of the Goldwater-Nichols Act in 1986, which gave the CJCS authority to act as an instrument of change. In the years since Goldwater-Nichols, the CJCS has frequently called for change to the UCP. General Powell (1989-1993) used his authority as CJCS to establish United States Strategic Command

---

[14] Ronald H. Cole, Walter S. Poole, et al., *The History of the Unified Command Plan 1946-1999* (Washington, DC: Joint History Office, Office of the Chairman of the Joint Chiefs of Staff, 2003), 26.
[15] Ibid., 1.

(USSTRATCOM), United States Atlantic Command (USACOM--later USJFCOM) and United States Transportation Command (USTRANSCOM) as fully competent functional commands.[16]

The CJCS also affects the UCP through the two primary documents. The first is the NMS. The NMS is the Chairman's comprehensive examination of U.S. military support to the national strategy. It provides an assessment of the security environment and identifies opportunities and challenges that affect U.S. national security. It also addresses the ends, ways, and means of the military strategy. Among those means considered are the combatant commands including their organization and employment of joint forces. The CJCS also has a statutory responsibility to conduct a review of the UCP "not less often than every two years" and submit recommended changes to the President, through the SecDef. This mandatory, biennial review enables the President and the SecDef to respond more effectively to the increasingly rapid evolution of "political and military realities."[17] In recent years, during UCP review principals have identified a number of conditions that must be met in order to propose changes to the UCP; chief among them is conformance with the NSS, NDS and public law.[18] As part of the review the CJCS must recommend to the President, through the SecDef, any necessary changes to the missions, responsibilities, or force structures. In addition to the CJCS, the Services and the combatant commanders also provide advice and input on any recommended changes. In the event of any differences or discrepancies, the CJCS serves as the final arbiter in resolving such differences. However, he is encouraged to forward any

---

[16] Ibid., 7.

[17] Ibid., 53.

[18] Story, *Military Changes to the Unified Command Plan: Background and Issues for Congress,* CRS-6.

dissenting views by the Service Chiefs to the SecDef and President for their consideration.

The Comprehensive Joint Assessment (CJA) is another document produced by the Chairman produces that has an influence on structure of the armed forces. The CJA is a formal, holistic strategic assessment process that provides a common informational baseline and strategic picture. The CJA provides a central unified mechanism for combatant commands and Services to describe the strategic environment, their opportunities, challenges, state of their organization, and overarching requirements.[19]

Congress

Although the UCP is an executive document, over the years Congress has acted on occasion to recommend changes to the UCP.[20] Congress has a vested interest in the DoD and the operations of the armed forces. Congressional involvement in matters of defense traces its roots to the U.S. Constitution. Article I, Section 8 of the Constitution enumerates the rights of the legislature and specifically authorizes Congress 'to provide for the common defense' as well as raise and support the armed forces.[21] Many congressional concerns regarding military integration and joint operations are addressed by and incorporated in military changes to the UCP. However, not all such concerns have been addressed by changes the military has instituted. On occasion, Congress has taken legislative action to accommodate certain interests and concerns[22] and these actions have directly and indirectly influenced the military and the UCP. Since the National

---

[19] Chairman of the Joint Chiefs of Staff Instruction (CJCSI) 3100.01B, Joint Strategic Planning System, dated December 12, 2008, p. A-6.

[20] Story, CRS-2.

[21] *The Constitution of the United States of America* (Philadelphia, PA: 1789), Article I, Section 8.

[22] Story, CRS-1.

Security Act of 1947, there have been a number of significant legislative initiatives passed that affect the authorities of the CJCS and combatant commanders or influenced the combatant command structure.[23] A summary of the major legislative initiatives follows:

- National Security Act of 1947 (Public Law 80-253, 26 July 1947) approved the first UCP and provided the legal foundation for the CJCS to create unified commands in strategic areas.

- DoD Reorganization Act of 1978 (Public Law 85-599, 6 August 1988) authorized the President through the SecDef to establish unified and specified commands, and assigned their missions and established force structures.

- Goldwater-Nichols DoD Reorganization Act of 1986 (Public Law 99-433) affected the UCP in a number of ways, including providing for the establishment of a unified transportation command and a biennial review by the CJCS of combatant command missions, responsibilities, force structure and geographic boundaries.

- 1987 SOCOM (Cohen/Daniel) Act (Public Law 99-661) was the result of Senator William Cohen and Representative Dan Daniel concerns that the Services were overlooking non-traditional and low-intensity conflict threats. Congress mandated establishment of U.S. Special Operations Command (SOCOM) as a separate specified command over the objections of the CJCS and combatant commanders.

---

[23] Story, CRS-7 thru 12.

- Commission on Roles and Missions of the Armed Forces National Defense Authorization Act for Fiscal Year 1994 (Public Law 103-160) recommended creation of a functional unified command responsible for joint training and integration of U.S. forces. U.S. Atlantic Command was relieved of its geographic area of responsibility and was redesignated as a functional command responsible for joint training, integration and joint force provider functions.

- National Defense Authorization Act for Fiscal Year 1997 (Public Law 104-201, Section 923) recommended a QDR to study U.S. defense strategy, modernization plans, force structures, and other defense programs and activities. It also contained a recommendation to significantly alter functional commands to incorporate new mission capabilities. This act created USJFCOM and added responsibility for joint experimentation to complement its joint training, joint force provider and joint integration missions.

Congress and the Base Realignment and Closure Process

Considering the history of congressional interest and involvement in national defense issues, it is not surprising the unilateral recommendation of the SecDef to close USJFCOM was met with shock, surprise and derision by Congressional leaders. In the days following the announcement, Virginia congressional leaders decried the Secretary's recommendation and questioned its legality.[24] The gravamen of their argument was that

---

[24]Kimball Payne, "Virginia Lawmakers Say Joint Forces Closure May be Illegal," *Newport News Daily Press*, August 12, 2010.

Secretary Gates "was attempting to skirt the traditionally rigorous base-closing process by claiming that the move is a 'work-force reduction' and not a full blown closing."[25]

Since the announcement of the closure of USJFCOM, there has been continued speculation concerning the issue and the interpretation of whether the command may or not fit into the legal framework of a base realignment and closure (BRAC) action. Title 10, U.S. Code, § 2687 specifies that no action may be taken to close any military installation in which at least 300 civilian personnel are authorized to be employed involving a reduction by more than 1,000 or by more than 50 percent in the number of civilian personnel authorized to be employed at such an installation without compliance with statutory provisions of Section 2687.[26] One such provision is the requirement to notify the Senate Armed Services Committee (SASC) and HASC. In the case of the Secretary's announcement regarding USJFCOM there was no prior notification to the HASC or SASC. The legal opinion of the DoD General Counsel is that the announced closure of USJFCOM is not a BRAC issue because its disestablishment[27] does not trigger the thresholds of Section 2687 - the disestablishment does not involve the closure of an installation or the realignment of any installation by more than 50% of the civilian personnel.[28] A considerable number of tenant organizations would still remain on the Naval Support Activity where the USJFCOM headquarters is located. Further,

---

[25] Payne, "Virginia Lawmakers Say Joint Forces Closure May Be Illegal."

[26] *Base Realignments and Closures*, 10 U.S.C. 2687, August 1, 1977 (with subsequent amendments) http://uscode.house.gov (accessed March 28, 2011).

[27] Author's note: Although the Secretary of SecDefe used the term "closure" in his announcement, subsequent discussions and open press articles have used the term "disestablishment". There is no doctrinal or legal difference in the terms. For consistency, the USJFCOM leadership uses the term disestablishment in its discussions with respect to the DoD efficiency initiatives.

[28] U.S. Joint Forces Command, "JFCOM Transition Information Site," https://us.jfcom.mil/sites/JTPT/Pages/Default.aspx (accessed December 23, 2010).

provisions of Section 2687 do not apply if the President certifies to the Congress that a closure or realignment must be implemented for reasons of national security or a military emergency. In the case of USJFCOM, the closure, it has not been attributed to national security or military emergency, so the BRAC issue is a moot point.

Congressional Actions since the Closure Announcement

In the months following the SecDef's announcement to close USJFCOM, there has been an escalation in congressional rhetoric on the issue. Immediately following, Secretary Gates' announcement, the Governor of Virginia and congressional leaders from the House and Senate–Democrats and Republicans–unanimously condemned the recommendation. Their concerns were motivated by perceptions that the SecDef's rationale for the closure was based on economics. The Virginia delegation demanded that a more thorough review be conducted of USJFCOM's mission and activities without a predisposed intent to close the command.

The Virginia lawmakers were concerned about the economic effects of disestablishing a major combatant command that employs thousands of personnel in well-paying jobs. Taking into account high unemployment across the nation, from their perspective the closure of USJFCOM would have a disastrous effect on the economy of southeastern Virginia. USJFCOM is an extremely vital component of the regional economy. Of the nearly 5,800 jobs, more than 3,900 are employed in the Hampton Roads region and an additional 5,100 jobs are created through indirect and induced effects.[29] Moreover, the presence of USJFCOM contributes over $700 million to the region's gross domestic product, $200 million in salaries and $500 million in defense

---

[29] Hampton Roads Planning District Commission, HRPDC Special Report "JFCOM Economic Impact Brief No1," August 19, 2010.

contracts awarded on an annual basis.[30] The Virginia congressional leaders were not

alone in their concern over the possible closure of the command. By the end of August,

Senator Carl Levin (D-MI), Chair of the SASC had agreed to hold full a committee

hearing on the recommendation to close USJFCOM. The hearing was held in September,

after Congress' summer recess.[31]

By early September, the HASC had added its voice to the chorus of those

questioning the wisdom of Secretary Gates' recommendation. Congressman Randy

Forbes (R-VA-04) announced that ranking members of the HASC had written to

Secretary Gates demanding information related to the legalities of the decision to close

USJFCOM. The HASC members requested a copy of all documents to include the DoD

General Counsel's legal opinion that concluded the closing of USJFCOM does not trigger

a BRAC action; a copy of the written recommendation provided by the Director of Cost

Assessment and Performance Evaluation with an analysis of the elements of the decision;

documents prepared by DoD that analyze the extent of savings in the department; and any

other pertinent materials.[32]

On 28 and 29 September 2010, the Senate and House hearings, respectively,

convened to consider the DoD Efficiencies Initiatives recommended by Secretary Gates.

The focus of the hearings considered the full range of initiatives outlined in the

Secretary's August 9, 2010 announcement; however, a review of the transcripts indicates

---

[30] Walter Pincus, "Joint Forces Command, Which Relies On Contractors, Is Tempting Target For Gates," *Washington Post*, August 18, 2010.

[31] Tracy Agnew," "Senate Review: Webb Secures Armed Services Committee Inquiry of JFCOM," *Suffolk News Herald*, August 25, 2010.

[32] Congressman Randy Forbes et al, House Committee on Armed Services to the Honorable Robert M. Gates, Secretary of Defense, August 31, 2010, http://forbes.house.gov/UploadedFiles/HPMForbesWittman_to_SecDef_re_Efficiencies.pdf (accessed December 23, 2010).

substantial concern over the decision to close USJFCOM and the topic dominated

discussions at the hearings. The senior DoD officials testifying at the hearings included

Deputy Secretary of Defense, William J. Lynn III; the Assistant Secretary of Defense for

Acquisition, Technology and Logistics, Dr. Ashton Carter; and Vice Chairman, JCS,

General James E. Cartwright, USMC. Testimony by DoD officials at the hearings

adduced that although detailed analysis was still ongoing, USJFCOM had outlived the

purpose for its creation and some missions and tasks performed by the command,

although vital, could be more effectively managed in a different place. USJFCOM had

made substantial progress on institutionalizing jointness within the combatant commands

and their operations; however, a four-star headquarters command with a budget

approaching $1 billion was no longer justified.[33] One example of a mission set identified

to be transferred from USJFCOM was joint manning or the joint force provider mission,

which witnesses asserted would best be handled at the Joint Staff.[34]

Despite the information presented at Senate and House hearings, members of

Congress continued to protest that their requests for detailed information and analysis on

the USJFCOM closure had still not been provided by the DoD. The HASC in a letter

dated October 7 to Secretary Gates advised it was unable to evaluate the rationale for

several of the decisions on defense efficiency initiatives without relevant documentation

and indicated the Committee would not provide either financial or legislative support for

---

[33] House Armed Services Committee, *Defense Department Efficiency Initiative,* 111th cong., 2nd sess., September 29, 2010. (http://democrats.armedservices.house.gov/index.cfm/2010/9/efficiencies (accessed December 23, 2010).

[34] U.S. Congress. Senate Armed Services Committee. "Holds Hearing on Defense Department Efficiencies Initiatives." (Date September 28, 2010). http://armed-services.senate.gov/Transcripts/2010/09%20September/10-72%20-%209-28-10.pdf (accessed December 23, 2010).

the decisions.[35] As congressional frustration over DoD reluctance to comply with

congressional requests reached its zenith, Senator James Webb (D-VA) placed a hold on

all Pentagon and military nominations until the DoD provided information he had been

seeking on the decision to shutter USJFCOM. Senator Webb identified the information

as "highly relevant" to Congress' ability to assess the proposal to shut down USJFCOM,

and "clearly within the congressional prerogative to ask for it."[36] Senator Webb asserted

that "proposals relating to major changes affecting unified commands should be guided

by a clear process, a sound analytical basis and compliance with applicable laws in a way

that everybody can understand it. The [DoD's] lack of transparency and consultation,

particularly with our [the Virginia] delegation, was in stark contrast to how these

decisions traditionally are made."[37] Senator Webb lifted the block on Senate

consideration of DoD nominations on November 18, 2010 after the Pentagon released

data that substantiated Secretary Gates' decision to close USJFCOM.[38]

On January 6, 2011, pursuant to his authority as Commander-in-Chief under Title

10 U.S.C., President Obama accepted the recommendation of Secretary Gates and in a

---

[35] Robert Brodsky, "Lawmakers Seek Justification for Closing Joint Forces Command," *Government Executive,* October 15, 2010.
http://www.govexec.com/story_page.cfm?filepath=/dailyfed/101510rb1.htm&oref=search (accessed December 23, 2010).

[36] Megan Scully, "Webb to Stall Future Defense Nominations Over JFCOM," *Government Executive,* October 26, 2010.
http://www.govexec.com/story_page.cfm?filepath=/dailyfed/1010/102610nj2.htm&oref=search (accessed December 23, 2010).

[37] Senator James Webb (D-VA), U.S. Congress. Senate Armed Services Committee. "Holds Hearing on Defense Department Efficiencies Initiatives." (Date September 28, 2010). http://armed-services.senate.gov/Transcripts/2010/09%20September/10-72%20-%209-28-10.pdf (accessed December 23, 2010).

[38] Roxana Tiron, "Webb Lifts Hold Over Nominees", *The Hill,* November 18, 2010. Available at:
http://thehill.com/homenews/senate/130019-webb-lifts-holds-over-military-nominees (accessed January 17, 2011).

Presidential memorandum formalized his approval of the disestablishment of USJFCOM

on a date to be determined by the SecDef.[39]

---

[39] Office of the White House Press Secretary, Memorandum for the Secretary of Defense, Disestablishment of United States Joint Forces Command, January 6, 2011.

CHAPTER 4:
THE CASE AGAINST CLOSURE

Previous chapters discussed U.S. Joint Forces Command's (USJFCOM's) organization and responsibilities, outlined the critical role the command plays in improving joint warfighting, and described the process for closing a combatant command and roles and responsibilities of major players. This chapter will make a case that aspects of USJFCOM's mission must endure and provide a rationale for continuing vital functions. Despite the dire financial challenges confronting the Department of Defense (DoD), it will argue that the Secretary of Defense's (SecDef's) decision to close USJFCOM is tantamount to "throwing the baby out with the bath water."

After nearly a decade at war in Operations ENDURING FREEDOM and IRAQI FREEDOM, the U.S. faces significant economic challenges and a growing budget deficit. The protracted nature of these irregular warfare and counterinsurgency operations has contributed heavily to the current fiscal burden. By 2010 annual discretionary spending was $583 billion above the level set in 2001 with defense spending accounting for nearly 65% of the increase.[1] During a time of heightened attention over federal deficits, all elements of the federal budget are under careful scrutiny. Accordingly, there has been a national debate on discretionary spending with a recommendation to significantly reduce DoD spending. In what may be perceived as cruel irony, the continued success and effectiveness of USJFCOM and the concomitant increase in the number of mission areas entrusted to them have combined to place them squarely in the crosshairs of the DoD

---

[1] Report of the Sustainable Defense Task Force, *"Debts, Deficits, and Defense: A Way Forward,"* (Washington, DC, June 11, 2010), v.

Efficiencies Task Force. Simply put, the command is "too successful and too big" as USJFCOM's achievements and the size of their staff were cited in briefings by Secretary Gates and the Defense Business Board (DBB). The DBB presentation depicted USJFCOM with estimates of 3,000 government (military/civilian) personnel and approximately 3,300 contractors.[2] The herculean size of the USJFCOM staff made them an easy target for reductions in comparison with the nine other combatant commands. Secretary Gates described USJFCOM as having largely outlived its usefulness to "infuse and compel jointness into everything the military does" and rationalized his analysis by citing two decades of operational experience in which the U.S. military has embraced jointness.[3] He also declared USJFCOM's four-star headquarters is an extra layer of bureaucracy whose benefits no longer outweighed the costs.

This author disagrees with Secretary Gates and contends that the wholesale closure of USJFCOM is analogous to throwing the baby out with the bath water. While there are a myriad of diverse activities carried out at USJFCOM, there are a number of core functions performed there with significant contributions to joint warfighting. Those core functions of USJFCOM must continue for a number of reasons. The principal arguments against closing USJFCOM are: 1) the decision was based on an inadequate cost benefit analysis; 2) USJFCOM's mission has not been accomplished and more work remains to be done; 3) jointness is not a naturally occurring phenomenon and requires nurturing; 4) the mandate for a joint force advocate; and 5) the SecDef's apparent

---

[2] Arnold Punaro, "Reducing Overhead and Improving Business Operations," Defense Business Board, Briefing, Public Session, July 22, 2010, slide 30. See also Figure III-1, above.

[3] Robert M. Gates, "Efficiencies Initiative".

acknowledgement that aspects of the command are vital and must endure. The rationale

supporting each of these reasons is detailed below.

The Case for USJFCOM

An Inadequate Cost-Benefit Analysis

The majority of DoD efficiencies introduced by Secretary Gates on August 9,

2010, and later approved by the President on January 6, 2010 are discerning and justified,

but the rationale for closing USJFCOM is incomplete. Although operating expenses have

increased substantially since the command's redesignation to USJFCOM in 1999,

USJFCOM's mission areas and span of control have also grown exponentially. The

mission creep occasioned by the additional responsibilities and authorities assigned to

USJFCOM through successive Unified Command Plan changes, and the many disparate

commands and activities resubordinated to them, have tripled the size of its staff in the

last decade.[4] In short, USJFCOM is a victim of its own success. As USJFCOM

significantly improved jointness along its core lines of operations, still other subordinate

commands and activities were migrated to USJFCOM under the rubric of improving

jointness. While the author agrees that reductions in the defense budget are necessary

and long overdue, any discussion or decision to close the command must be predicated

on sound analysis and with a clear understanding of the benefit in terms of projected cost

savings. In evaluating the argument for closing USJFCOM, the DBB study was long on

recommendations yet offered no detailed estimate of costs savings. Although the board's

principal task was to identify efficiencies, its presentation stopped short of identifying

any efficiency to be gained by the closure of USJFCOM or providing any business case

---

[4] William J. Lynn, Deputy Secretary of Defense, on September 29, 2010, before the House Armed Services
Committee, 111th Congress, 2nd sess.
http://democrats.armedservices.house.gov/index.cfm/2010/9//efficiencies (accessed December 23, 2010).

analysis setting forth the merits of their recommendation. An attempt to acquire and examine the business case analysis from the DBB was unsuccessful because there was no business case analysis involved in their recommendation to close the command.[5]

Secretary Gates' rationale for the closure cited economic factors and a perception that the Services' operational experiences of the past two decades render obsolete any requirement to instill jointness across the Services. He asserts that USJFCOM has "outlived its usefulness." Setting aside for the moment a discussion on the usefulness of USJFCOM, the Secretary's economic argument appears financially sound. Moreover, it is refreshing to learn–after a mere five months of study by the DoD Efficiencies Task Force–that the DoD will save approximately $400 million a year by dismantling USJFCOM.[6] Even though the cost saving appears to be significant, it represents only four tenths of one percent (.04%) of the $100 billion dollar savings sought by Secretary Gates. A fuller appreciation of the cost benefit analysis is not feasible until the detailed plan to implement the decision is made available.

On a purely economic basis, the recommendation to trim defense spending is not without merit, but it is difficult to appreciate the benefits of the decision to close USJFCOM beyond the short-term horizon of a five-year term, e.g., the future years defense program (FYDP) budget of 2012-2016. The SecDef's decision to close USJFCOM is short-sighted and imprudent–save now, pay later. In return for short-term cost savings, there is no mention or consideration of the long-term implications for the

---

[5] CAPT Michael Bohn, USN, Military Assistant to the Defense Business Board, e-mail message to the author, January 18, 2011. Author's note: Responding to the author's query for business case analysis supporting the DBB recommendation to close USJFCOM, CAPT Bohn replied there is no business case analysis.

[6] Bill Bartel, "JFCOM Will Shut Down in about 10 Months, Commander Says," *Virginian Pilot*, January 11, 2011.

U.S. armed forces or the unintended consequences that may accrue to defense capabilities from the decision such as regression in the area of jointness by the Services.

Further, regardless of the SecDef's intentions to trim costs and reinvest in force structure and modernization, there is little guarantee that the administration and members of Congress will allow the DoD to keep the savings. That caution was voiced in a committee hearing on Defense Efficiencies Initiatives. Ranking Member of the House, Armed Services Committee, Representative Howard "Buck" McKeon (R-CA) testified that during the summer of 2010, the White House supported a teacher bailout which was financed in part with savings from DoD. The DoD savings were projected to remedy a shortage in the Navy's military pay accounts. When the payroll monies were lost, the Navy was required to move money from aircraft procurement accounts, which in turn postponed an upgrade to training simulators and deferred the purchase of external fuel tanks for the F/A-18 Super Hornet fleet.[7]

Challenges Remain – USJFCOM's Work is Not Finished

The SecDef asserts that USJFCOM is no longer required to instill jointness in the military Services. The inference drawn from this logic is that the U.S. military has crossed the *jointness finish line* and further joint doctrine, joint education, or joint training and exercises are superfluous. Secretary Gates' assertion is a logical fallacy of the false cause variety. The fallacy results from arriving at a conclusion without taking into consideration other factors that may bear on the matter. Although there have been

---

[7] Representative Howard "Buck" P. McKeon (R-CA), Ranking Member House, Armed Services Committee, on September 29, 2010, before the House Armed Services Committee, 111th Congress, 2nd sess. http://democrats.armedservices.house.gov/index.cfm/2010/9//efficiencies (accessed December 23, 2010).

great strides in the past fifteen years in the attainment of a more joint force, that progress is a transitory condition. Jointness is not a goal to be attained and once attained ignored. A more accurate analogy is that jointness is a journey and not a destination. The journey requires steady progress to arrive at the intended end state. Although progress along the road to jointness may be measured through achievement of joint training standards and a mastery of joint mission essential task lists, evolution towards jointness is a continuing action–just as security, camouflage, and protection of the force in a combat zone are continuing actions. The lack of a concerted and focused effort to advance joint military operations endangers the ability of the Services to harmonize their efforts towards a common purpose and imperils the benefits of joint warfare. In a worst case scenario, it could result in failed or less-than-satisfactory military operations, such as Operation EAGLE CLAW (1981)[8] and Operation URGENT FURY (1983).[9] Those operational disasters created the environment that led to the passage of the Goldwater-Nichols Act of 1986.

The SecDef's contention that USJFCOM is no longer necessary is premature. The decision to close USJFCOM is abandoning a decades-long effort initiated to ensure maximum effectiveness of the U.S. military and supported by multiple SecDefs and Chairmen of the Joint Chiefs of Staff. There are twelve years of public testimony and written analysis espousing improvements in the joint force and the work of USJFCOM in mandating jointness across the Services through improvements in joint training, doctrine,

---

[8] Charles A. Nemfakos, Irv Blickstein, et al, *Perfect Storm: The Goldwater-Nichols Act and its Effect on Navy Acquisition* (RAND Corporation, 2010), 8. Operation EAGLE CLAW was the failed attempt to rescue the Iranian hostages from the U.S. Embassy in Iran.

[9] Ibid., 8. Operation URGENT FURY was an ad hoc joint operation, the invasion of Grenada, to oust a Cuban-sponsored People's Revolutionary Government and to protect U.S. citizens. The operation was plagued by poor intelligence, inefficient joint logistics support and communications interoperability problems.

concept development and experimentation, and joint standards development. Any

progress measured against the attainment of jointness can be attributed principally to two

factors which have combined to compel the acceptance of jointness: 1) USJFCOM's

decade as the joint force advocate or "bridge-builder" amongst the Services to inculcate

jointness and inspire cooperation in areas such as joint training and joint interoperability;

and 2) the external pressures of combat during Operations ENDURING FREEDOM and

IRAQI FREEDOM which have largely removed most of the existing Service rivalries

and parochialisms at the tactical and operational levels out of necessity. The necessity

principle states that jointness tends to increase on the lower echelons of command in the

face of the enemy. The supreme lesson of the Pacific War was that true unity of

command could be achieved only on the field of battle.[10] A crisis on the order of war, or

an operation conducted under the rubric of national defense, increases the likelihood that

compromise will be achieved and a consensus can be reached. Since a common unifying

goal is important to achieving unity of effort, it enables a coalition to form to clarify or

re-state goals; differences often revolve around the ways or means.

Nurture versus Nature

Jointness is not a natural phenomenon. It does not operate as a well-oiled

machine. Organization has traditionally been a deficiency of our national defense

throughout American history. The Army and Navy disputes of the early 20th century

were not able to be remedied during World War II. It was only after the conclusion of

the war that Congress stepped in to settle the dispute with the passage of the National

---

[10] Robert C. Rubel, "Principles of Jointness", *Joint Forces Quarterly*, (Winter 2000-01), 46. Note: In this article Rubel tries to examine the comprehensive theory that underpins jointness by examining a number of complementary principles. Rubel also cited a study by Louis Morton, "Pacific Command: A Study in Inter-service Relations", The Harmon Memorial Lectures in Military History, 1957-1987, (Washington: Office of Air Force History, 1988), 152.

Security Act of 1947.[11] Despite the changes mandated by the Act, reorganization efforts over the next forty years yielded only marginal progress towards resolving the inter-service squabbling. This lack of progress paved the way for Congressional action once again and the Goldwater-Nichols DoD Reorganization Act of 1986 was developed and passed. As testament to the recalcitrance and parochialism of the Services, the bitter and protracted battle over the passage of the Goldwater-Nichols legislation pitted two former allies, Congress and the Services, against each other and lasted for four years and 241 days–a longer period than U.S. involvement in World War II.[12]

Joint warfare is team warfare. While reaching consensus on shared goals is an important prerequisite–consensus must be constantly nurtured which is much more difficult if goals are not clear or change over time.[13] Although the Goldwater-Nichols Act directed the Services to work together and emphasized joint operations, the mere passage of that landmark legislation did not immediately resolve the problem. The problem is straightforward. Individual Service members, and in general the Services, view the world through their own lenses. Their differing missions, operational environments or domains, experiences and training all lead to different perspectives. These divergent perspectives fuel Service parochialism and foster inter-Service rivalry.[14] Joint culture within the DoD comes at the expense of the Services. As conflicts arose over finite resources, intra-Service rivalry increased and Service parochialism emerged.

---

[11] James R. Locher III, "Has it Worked? The Goldwater-Nichols Reorganization Act," *Naval War College Review* 54, no. 4 (Autumn 2001): 1.

[12] Ibid., 2.

[13] Joint Advanced Warfighting School, *Operational Art and Campaigning Primer AY10-11*, (Norfolk, VA: Joint Forces Staff College) 3: 51.

[14] Dennis M. Drew, "Jointness the Fundamental Problem: A Review of Joint Pub 1," *Airpower Journal* 6, No. 2 (Summer 1992): 59.

At the end of the day, each Service is involved in an existential battle for resources against the others.[15] The twelfth CJCS, General Colin Powell, recognized the cultural bias existing within the Services, the imbalance between Service and joint interests, and designated U.S. Atlantic Command, the predecessor to USJFCOM, to function as the joint force integrator because he believed that continental based U.S. forces were Service-oriented.[16]

Mandate for a Joint Force Advocate

General Powell's designation of a joint force advocate was inspired by his observations and experiences of the Operations DESERT SHIELD and DESERT STORM.[17] A full five years after the passage of the Goldwater-Nichols Act after action reports, lessons learned and studies of operations from the first Gulf War identified challenges in joint operations and interoperability. Michael R. Gordon and Bernard E. Trainor in their book, *The General's War,* highlighted several instances of Service bias as a causal factor in the failure to evolve towards jointness during the campaign.[18] Component commanders were given free rein to develop their plans during the buildup prior to the invasion of Kuwait making it difficult to develop a unified plan from the conflicting Service plans. The development of the air campaign did not involve the embarked naval component command staff which generated disagreement by Navy

---

[15] Anthony H. Cordesman, *Reforming Defense Decisionmaking: Taking Responsibility and Making Meaningful Plans* (Washington, DC: Center for Strategic and International Studies Report, March 11, 2009). http://csis.org/print/5166 (accessed January 10, 2011).

[16] Ronald H. Cole, Walter S. Poole, et al., *The History of the Unified Command Plan 1946-1999* (Washington, DC: Joint History Office, Office of the Chairman of the Joint Chiefs of Staff, 2003), 6.

[17] Author's note: Operations DESERT SHIELD and DESERT STORM were the principal U.S. and coalition operations to repel the Iraqi invasion of Kuwait and restore the territorial integrity of Kuwait. The operations were conducted in 1990 and 1991.

[18] Michael R. Gordon and Bernard E. Trainor, *The Generals' War: The Inside Story of the Conflict in the Gulf* (Boston: Little, Brown and Company, 1995), 186-7.

planners on the rules of engagement and over how air operations would be executed.[19] Additionally, the initial offensive ground strategy developed by Army planners excluded Marine Corps input and relegated them to a minor role. These are only a few examples, but there were a number of areas in which military operations were negatively affected by either competition between the Services or insufficient coordination among them. The most dangerous results were the friendly fire incidents, which involved Air Force planes mistakenly targeting Army and Marine ground forces.[20]

Having no joint force advocate is an impediment to efficient military operations and threatens U.S. national security. United States national experience has shown that it works best when someone is vested with the responsibility and authority to manage the process. There must be someone to integrate, synchronize and coordinate across the military. The fourteenth CJCS, General Hugh Shelton, cemented the joint force advocate's authority to compel jointness amongst the services and combatant commands by redesignating U.S. Atlantic Command as USJFCOM. The re-designation was promulgated in the Unified Command Plan (UCP) of 1999. Subsequent versions of the UCP have strengthened and clarified the functions of USJFCOM. USJFCOM has not dictated cooperation among engaged defense agencies, Services, and combatant commanders. However, working together over the past decade on lines of operations such as joint training, joint force interoperability and integration, and joint experimentation, the command has nurtured a cooperative spirit of jointness among all participants. This continued nurturing of the joint force must endure in order to comply

---

[19] Richard Weitz, "Jointness and Desert Storm: A Retrospective," *Defense and Security Analysis* 20, no. 2, (June 2004): 136.

[20] Ibid., 141. Approximately 25% of all U.S. casualties during DESERT STORM resulted from friendly fire.

with the mandate in the National Military Strategy 2004, "to enhance the ability to fight as a joint force. Joint teamwork is an integral part of our culture and focus as we develop leaders, organizations, systems and doctrine. We must continue to strengthen trust and confidence among the Service components that comprise the Joint Force."[21]

The Secretary's About Face

Between the SecDef's August 2010 recommendation to close USJFCOM and the Presidential approval in January 2011, Secretary Gates must have experienced a change of heart. In the span of five short months, the Secretary wavered between *close* and *downsize,* and eventually concluded that *50% of the command should remain.* This change of heart is consistent with the Secretary's earlier caution against regressing in the area of jointness mentioned in his August 2010 recommendation to close USJFCOM. While the reason for the SecDef's reversal of position regarding closure of the command is not known, it is likely the result of a combination of factors including five months of detailed study by DoD and Joint Staff Efficiencies Task Forces and an analysis of USJFCOM's core functions. At the conclusion of those study deliberations, the SecDef retained approximately 50% of USJFCOM's core competencies intact. Another supporting factor may be Secretary Gates' recollection and realization of the myriad of critical functions he observed during his official visit and tour of USJFCOM shortly after he began his tenure as SecDef.

In February 2007, Secretary Gates visited USJFCOM and received briefings on USJFCOM missions and functions and a tour of the facilities.[22] During Gates'

---

[21] Chairman of the Joint Chiefs of Staff, National Military Strategy of the U.S.–A Strategy for Today; A Vision for Tomorrow, Washington, DC: 2004, iv.

[22] Leo P. Hirrel, *US Joint Forces Command Historical Report, November 2005 to November 2007,* (Norfolk, VA: U.S. Joint Forces Command, 2009), 174.

orientation visit the Secretary commented to his escort, then USJFCOM Deputy Commander, Lieutenant General Woods, on several occasions "that he had no idea, absolutely no idea" of the breadth and depth of USJFCOM responsibilities.[23] Although Secretary Gates was very familiar with USJFCOM's joint force provider function because of the Secretary's role in the global force management process, he was completely unfamiliar with the detailed work that USJFCOM had accomplished in the joint training, experimentation and other enabling capability areas.

Summary

Secretary Gates is to be commended for his leadership in realizing that unlimited defense spending must be held in check. However, the approach taken regarding the decision to close USJFCOM is analogous to the misguided marksmanship philosophy of "*ready, fire, aim.*" The decision to close USJFCOM was announced prematurely without an analysis to determine costs, benefits or consequences of the decision. By unilaterally proceeding without the involvement or engagement of Congress, Secretary Gates' decision has left him open to criticism from Congress, the local community and defense industries. Ultimately Gates' decision to retain approximately 50% of USJFCOM capabilities in place indicates that the Secretary was persuaded of the vital work happening at the command and the need to retain a number of critical functions and resubordinate them to another organization. The next chapter will discuss which aspects of USJFCOM should endure and make a recommendation for their placement.

---

[23] LTG John Wood, USA, Deputy Commander, U.S. Joint Forces Command, interview by Leo P. Hirrel, September 10, 2008. (Norfolk, VA: Office of the Command Historian, U.S. Joint Forces Command).

CHAPTER 5:
DON'T THROW THE BABY OUT WITH THE BATH WATER

This chapter will discuss options for moving forward with implementation of the Presidential directive to close USJFCOM. This chapter will not recommend a specific course of action or methodology for closing USJFCOM; however, it will present a case that aspects of USJFCOM's mission must endure and evaluate where those responsibilities should be placed if the command is closed. The complete and wholesale closure of USJFCOM without regard for some of the vital functions carried out there will have deleterious effects on present and future warfighting abilities. The Secretary of Defense's (SecDef's) recommendation to eliminate USJFCOM, made as it was without any specific analysis or guidance, leaves open the possibility of throwing the baby out with the bath water. In analyzing the major Unified Command Plan (UCP) functions assigned to USJFCOM, the author identifies three that are deemed critical to promoting jointness. Joint force sourcing and management, joint force training and exercises, and joint integrator missions are the three most vital USJFCOM functions that must endure.

What Should Endure

In considering the future of joint warfighting there are a number of mission areas currently assigned to USJFCOM that must endure. Admittedly, an argument could be made for continuing any of the six mission areas, but from the author's perspective the three most vital functions are those which have been assigned to the command (and its predecessors) since the early 1990s: the joint force provider and joint training and exercise mission areas assigned in 1993, and the joint integrator role assigned in 1998. A supporting rationale for each of these three mission areas will be discussed in this section.

Joint Force Provider

Even advocates for the demise of USJFCOM understand and recognize that many operational commanders view the most important function of USJFCOM as the joint force provider mission.[1] USJFCOM has been a linchpin in the global force management process as almost 80% of continental-United States based forces are assigned to them by the Forces for Unified Commands Memorandum and the Global Force Management Implementation Guidance.[2] Combatant commands submit requests for forces (RFFs), which are reviewed and authenticated by the Joint Staff and passed to USJFCOM for sourcing. In furtherance of the force provider mission, USJFCOM coordinates with its Service component commands to marry up capabilities to each requirement. This process requires extensive coordination to craft a joint force solution from the pool of available conventional forces. That the function has been coordinated by USJFCOM for almost two decades is testament to the success of the process. The Joint Staff serving as the validation authority provides a level of inquiry and analysis for each requirement. This two-step process assures that all requirements are thoroughly vetted and deemed justifiable before forwarding to the SecDef for approval.

In carrying out its force provider responsibilities, USJFCOM coordinates with its component commands, U.S. Fleet Forces Command (FLTFORCOM); Marine Forces Command (MARFORCOM); Air Combat Command (ACC) , and U.S. Forces Command (FORSCOM). Only the Army component command, FORSCOM, is located outside the

---

[1] Robert Brackell, "Joint Force Provider," The New Atlanticist Policy and Analysis Blog, entry posted February 11, 2011, http://www.acus.org/new_atlanticist/joint-force-provider (accessed February 23, 2011).

[2] Author's Note: Forces and resources placed under a combatant commander by the Secretary of Defense in his "Forces for Unified Commands" memorandum, in conjunction with Global Force Management Implementation Guidance (GFMIG), are available for normal peacetime operations of that command.

southeastern Virginia area. The close proximity of three of the four component

commands is crucial to establishing working relationships amongst the principals and is

beneficial in coordinating the minute details of directing, scheduling and controlling the

inter-theater deployments of force packages bound for a combatant command operating

on the other side of the globe. Among the more highly visible force provider missions

coordinated by USJFCOM has been the sourcing of the additional 30,000 troops for the

surge in Afghanistan.[3] In late 2009 and early 2010, USJFCOM coordinated three force

packages responding to a request for forces from the Commander, U.S. Forces,

Afghanistan, which were ultimately approved by the Commander-in-Chief, President

Obama. The joint force capability is crucial for the effective global force management of

and must be retained by the successor organization to USJFCOM as the debate over

which functions must endure is played out within DoD.

Joint Force Integration

The U.S. military must improve and increase effectiveness by joining with other

organizations and forces to unify and integrate efforts to achieve jointness. A major

enabler of joint integration is a new level of interoperability and systems that are

developed jointly; i.e., designed and conceptualized with joint architectures and

acquisition strategies.[4] USJFCOM has been working since 1999 with the Services, the

Joint Staff and DoD to introduce jointness into the capability development process. The

end states of these efforts are improved equipment and systems that are interoperable

---

[3] Jacob Boyer, "USJFCOM Force Planners Play Vital Role in Force Deployment," *USJFCOM Public Affairs Office*, December 8, 2009. http://www.jfcom.mil/newslink/storyarchive/2009/pa120809.html (accessed February 23, 2011).

[4] Chairman of the Joint Chiefs of Staff, *National Military Strategy of the U.S.–A Strategy for Today; A Vision for Tomorrow*, (Washington, DC: Joint Chiefs of Staff, 2004), 15.

across the Services, but also cost considerably less to develop and field. One area that has seen improvement is the Blue Force Tracker developed through a USJFCOM initiative. When U.S. forces first deployed overseas to Iraq and Afghanistan, the Services had different and incompatible systems in use to track "blue" or friendly forces.[5] The USJFCOM solution employs a satellite communication network to provide detailed information on friendly and enemy units which lessens the possibility of fratricide and improves battlefield coordination. The lesson from this example is to begin with the end in mind; to meet warfighter needs and minimize gaps in capabilities from the tactical level through interface with the strategic levels, interoperability must be kept in mind during the development of the system. Without USJFCOM this integration would never have occurred.

Interoperable systems don't magically occur because everyone signs up to jointness.[6] There must be a continuing requirement to monitor integration of new and existing Service systems to ensure that individual program offices are informed of ongoing efforts in related capabilities being developed and fielded. Systems must be born joint and a joint force advocate must be designated to compel the integration. Another important aspect of joint integration is the joint doctrine which promotes a common perspective from which to plan, train and conduct military operations. Doctrine represents what is taught, believed, and advocated as what is right. It presents fundamental principles that guide the employment of forces in coordinated and integrated

---

[5] Donna Miles, "Jointness Becomes Key Focus in Developing Military Capability," *American Forces Press Service*, March 14, 2006. http://www.globalsecurity.org/military/library/news/2006/03/mil-060314-afps02.htm (accessed February 23, 2010).

[6] Bob Killebrew, "Goodbye, JFCOM," *Armed Forces Journal*, November 2010. http://www.armedforcesjournal.com/2010/11/4783736 (accessed February 23, 2011).

action toward a common objective.[7]

Joint Force Training and Exercises

For the joint force to function effectively there must be a high degree of mutual trust. Mutual trust results from honest efforts by the individual Service member to learn about and understand the capabilities that each member brings to the joint force, demonstrated competence in planning, and training together.[8] As the Chairman of the Joint Staff's (CJCS's) lead agent for joint training, USJFCOM provides trained and ready conventional military forces and staffs to other commands, as directed, and serves as the primary joint force provider. This joint force trainer responsibility underscores the recognition that joint training of U.S. military forces requires some measure of standardization. The Joint Warfighting Center (J7) is USJFCOM's principal trainer with the mission to support combatant commander training across the spectrum of individual, staff and collective training.[9]

As the Joint Force Trainer, USJFCOM is committed to supporting two prioritized exercises for each combatant commander and one Joint Staff Eligible Receiver series exercise per year.[10] One important example is the series of Unified Endeavor (UE) exercises conducted to train combined-joint task force (CJTF) commanders and their staffs operating in complex operations. UE is a mission rehearsal exercise (MRX) employing modeling and simulation capabilities to replicate a realistic environment to

---

[7] Joint Chiefs of Staff, *Unified Action Armed Forces (UNAAF)*, Joint Publication 0-2 (Washington DC: Joint Chiefs of Staff, May 2, 2007, w/ change 1 of 20 March 2009), ix.

[8] Joint Chiefs of Staff, *Doctrine for the Armed Forces of the U.S.*, Joint Publication 1 (Washington DC: Joint Chiefs of Staff, May 2, 2007, incorporating change 1 of March 20, 2009), IV-18.

[9] Chairman of the Joint Chiefs of Staff, *Joint Training Manual for the Armed Forces of the United States*, CJCSM 3500.03B, Washington, DC: Joint Chiefs of Staff, current as of August 15, 2008). http://www.dtic.mil/cjcs_directives/cdata/unlimit/m350003.pdf (accessed February 23, 2010)

[10] Ibid., Q-2. (Author's note: Eligible Receiver is a no-notice interoperability exercise designed to practice interagency response to crisis situations; generally focused on counterterrorism.)

train staffs for their missions in preparation for their deployments to Afghanistan, Iraq or the Horn of Africa. The MRX is complemented by a tailored academic review session to focus the unit on the mission of a CJTF which includes best practices and an orientation to lessons learned by prior units. Usually two-to-three months after the conclusion of the MRX, a staff assistance visit (SAV) is conducted while the unit is executing its command responsibilities in theater. The SAV affords an opportunity to continue the development of the staff as it executes its assigned or anticipated missions. The exercise programs developed by USJFCOM, and coordinated in its Joint Warfighting Center, stress cultural awareness and the decision-making skills for success in conflict. This is an essential program that is enabling the success of the joint warfighter deployed in combat environments.[11] This program must remain an enduring requirement as the U.S. military forces will be committed in Afghanistan and Iraq for at least the next few years.

The Best Fit for the Job

Having identified specific functional areas of USJFCOM that must endure, it is apparent that some vestige of the command must continue. If USJFCOM will not survive beyond the end of fiscal year 2011, it is worth considering where the enduring critical functions will reside. The potential list of candidates for assignment of these responsibilities is a select group comprised of the Joint Staff, the Services or a combatant command. This section will consider the merits of assigning the responsibilities to each of these three organizations.

Joint Staff

The Joint Staff works for the CJCS and their actions support the Chairman in

---

[11] General James N. Mattis, Commander, USJFCOM, on March 10, 2010, before the House Armed Services Committee, 111th Congress, 2nd sess.

carrying out his Title 10, U.S.C. responsibilities to oversee the Armed Forces and advise the President, the SecDef and the National Security Council. The Joint Staff as an organization is involved in policy-related matters for the combatant commands, but the Joint Staff concentrates at the strategic level. It doesn't traditionally venture into the combatant command arena of operational level issues. The Defense Reform Initiative of 1997 transferred a number of formerly Chairman-controlled activities from the Joint Staff to then USLANTCOM (later USACOM then USJFCOM) because the command was a better fit for those operational level training and doctrine responsibilities. While the Joint Staff did maintain a policy, resource allocation, or monitoring role of those activities, the Joint Staff was ill-suited for their operational-level focus.[12] At the time of their transfer to USJFCOM, the Joint Staff also transferred approximately 12% of their military billets (170 of 1400) to USJFCOM. Clearly, there is a role for the Joint Staff, but that role should be limited to its current responsibilities of policy and oversight.

Services

The Services are likewise vested with Title 10 U.S.C. responsibilities. Their specific authorities are to recruit, train, organize and equip their forces to participate as part of the larger joint force. It is not sufficient to be adept in Service skills because the paradigm for operations is a joint operating environment. Increasingly, there is a need to staff the joint headquarters and perform in joint and coalition contexts–wholly foreign to the routine duties of the Services. This argues for joint competencies that need to be built upon the foundation of Service-level competencies. Doctrine should be shaped by both operational experience and an understanding of the future challenges. Joint capability

---

[12] William S. Cohen, Defense Reform Initiative Report, Washington, DC: Office of the Secretary of Defense, November 1997, Appendix C-7. http://www.fas.org/man/docs/dri/cover.htm (accessed June 13, 2011).

requirements should also reflect the operational perspective. This is not a task or mission for any of the Services. Although individual Service members may understand the philosophy, their principal focus is on their service specific capabilities, and rightfully so. Chapter 4 examined the negative effects of parochialism and the necessity for an independent joint advocate to manage and synchronize efforts across all the Services. Nearly 20 years after the passage of Goldwater-Nichols Act, General Tommy Franks, former Commander, U.S. Central Command (USCENTCOM), described the four Service Chiefs during the planning for Operation IRAQI FREEDOM as more concerned with their Services' parochial interests than working together to win a war.[13] In consideration of these factors, the Services should not be assigned the responsibilities for continuing the joint work previously undertaken by USJFCOM.

Combatant Commands

The role of the joint force advocate is to be an honest broker and keep a watchful eye on the joint force customer–that is the commander who overseas joint activities and commands joint forces, whether a combatant commander or a joint task force commander.[14] USJFCOM has capably filled the role of joint force advocate for nearly twenty years. Although reviews of USJFCOM's performance may have been mixed, there were no accusations of favoritism or preferential treatment of one combatant command over another. In the 21st century, it is widely accepted as self-evident that all combatant commands are not created equal. The size and scope of areas of responsibility, resources apportioned to then, and the protracted nature of operations in

---

[13] Bob Woodward, *Plan of Attack*, (New York: Simon and Schuster, 2004), 118-119.

[14] LTG John Wood, USA, Deputy Commander, U.S. Joint Forces Command, interview by Leo P. Hirrel, September 10, 2008. (Norfolk, VA: Office of the Command Historian, U.S. Joint Forces Command).

southwest Asia have combined to favor U.S. Pacific Command and USCENTCOM as unofficial *firsts among equals* in the ranks of combatant commands. This joint force advocate responsibility should not be vested in a geographic combatant commander, as it might engender a potential conflict of interest favoring one combatant commander over another. In order for a joint force advocate to build credibility and display an understanding of combatant commander needs, it is important that a disinterested third party be designated as the joint force advocate.

Summary

As highlighted above, there are a number of functions currently assigned to USJFCOM that have strategic consequences if not continued. The decision to close USJFCOM appears to have been hastily made without a fair consideration of the effects of its closure. If USJFCOM is closed, responsibility for those joint functional areas must be vested elsewhere. After examining three principal candidates, the author concedes that although the Joint Staff may not the ideal place to vest these responsibilities, it is better positioned to take over the responsibilities with the least disruption to the joint warfighting community. Accordingly, the author recommends the former USJFCOM responsibilities should be assigned the Joint Staff. Although the Joint Staff is focused at the strategic level, and the enduring USJFCOM mission areas are more reflective of operational level initiatives, the Joint Staff already has an oversight role in many of these areas which supports transfer of responsibility for them to the Joint Staff. Moreover, as the functions are already being performed in Norfolk, Virginia, the author cautions that moving them physically to another venue may prove disruptive and recommends leaving them in place.

CHAPTER 6:
CONCLUSIONS AND RECOMMENDATIONS

This paper has argued against the Secretary's decision to close U.S. Joint Forces Command (USJFCOM). Although the stated reason to close the command was described as a *military decision* and not a *business case analysis*,[1] from the SecDef's apparent emphasis on achieving efficiencies and costs savings in order to maintain force structure and modernize equipment, it appears the decision was motivated principally by economic considerations. At a time of growing concern over federal deficits, all elements of the federal budget must undergo careful scrutiny. The Pentagon's budget should be no exception. As Secretary Gates has previously remarked, paraphrasing President Dwight D. Eisenhower, "The United States should spend as much as necessary on national defense, but not one penny more."[2] It is laudable to be concerned with budgetary savings given the state of the federal budget deficit;[3] however, the decision to shutter USJFCOM without regard for other than economic factors has the potential to reverse the past twenty years' developments in military effectiveness. With deference to the leadership of the Department of Defense (DoD), the decision to close USJFCOM seems shortsighted. While the cost of an additional four-star headquarters is not justifiable, the author contends that complete closure of USJFCOM should not occur for three reasons: 1) the decision to close the command was based on flawed logic; 2) the closure imperils the

---

[1] House Armed Services Committee, *Defense Department Efficiency Initiative,* 111th cong., 2nd sess., September 29, 2010. (http://democrats.armedservices.house.gov/index.cfm/2010/9/efficiencies) (accessed December 23, 2010).

[2] *Report of the Tenth Quadrennial Review of Military Compensation, Volumes I & II* (Fort Belvoir: Defense Technical Information Center, February 2008).

[3] Elizabeth C. Delisle, Barbara Edwards, et al., *Monthly Budget Review Fiscal Year 2010: A Congressional Budget Office Analysi*s (Washington, DC: Congressional Budget Office, October 7, 2010) (http://www.cbo.gov/ftpdocs/119xx/doc11936/SeptemberMBR.pdf (accessed January 21, 2011). The CBO estimated the federal budget in fiscal year 2010 at slightly less than $1.3 billion.

future and long-term success of future military operations; and 3) the unilateral nature and lack of transparency of the decision. A brief discussion of the major points underpinning the three reasons follows.

The SecDef's rationale for closing USJFCOM is faulty. He asserted USJFCOM had outlived its usefulness, citing the past two decades of joint operational experience. The SecDef's contention is based on a perspective of the Services in 2010 and does not take into consideration the ephemeral or fleeting nature of jointness. The condition must be continually nurtured by an impartial joint force advocate. Attempts at joint operations and coordination fail due to a lack of joint perspectives, staff continuity, and an inadequate appreciation for the need of institutionalized coordination processes, and joint education and training. A joint force advocate is needed to serve as an honest broker for the DoD. This responsibility cannot be vested in a *lead Service* because of the diverse, and sometimes competing, interests of individual Services. The principal purpose for creation of USJFCOM was to force a service-centric military culture to embrace joint operations and doctrine.[4]

The decision to close USJFCOM is short-sighted and threatens the future of joint military operations and effectiveness. When closure was initially recommended, no specific analysis was introduced which justified the decision or addressed potential long-term effects. While the past decade of operations in Iraq and Afghanistan have demonstrated considerable progress towards jointness, how will the next generation of sergeants, captains, and colonels currently rising through the ranks achieve it? As the

---

[4] Senate Armed Services Committee, *Defense Department Efficiency Initiative,* 111th cong., 2nd sess., September 28, 2010. http://armed-services.senate.gov/Transcripts/2010/09%20September/10-72%-%209-28-10.pdf (accessed December 23, 2010).

United States' history has shown, Service parochialism has frequently resulted in congressional action to spur the services to drink from the trough of jointness.

The U.S. Congress deserved an opportunity to review the decision. As discussed earlier in Chapter 3, the process for closing a combatant command is a highly contentious issue involving a number of parties and contemplation of a number of factors. In the decision to close USJFCOM, the decision was reached without the benefit of congressional participation or oversight. Information and analysis supporting the decision to close USJFCOM were withheld from Congress until mid-November despite formal requests by members of the House and Senate Armed Services Committees and congressional hearings on the DoD efficiencies. During the September 28, 2010, hearing of the House, Armed Services Committee, the Chairman and Ranking Member expressed "skepticism in the secretive nature of the DoD discussions on the closure of USJFCOM". Still another committee member expressed disdain over "90 days of [DoD] backroom meetings without one scintilla of evidence" offered as analysis for the basis to close the USJFCOM [by a single DoD witness at the hearing].[5] Based on a review of the transcripts, the magnitude of the decision to close a combatant command, and the potentially far-reaching effects of the decision, congressional leaders should have had an opportunity to consult on the issue and participate in the debate. An inclusive approach involving Congress was necessary in order to ensure an informed decision based on a full

---

[5] House Armed Services Committee, *Defense Department Efficiency Initiative,* 111th cong., 2nd sess., September 29, 2010. (http://democrats.armedservices.house.gov/index.cfm/2010/9/efficiencies) (accessed December 23, 2010). Author's note: Representative Ike Skelton, (D-MO) and Representative Howard P. "Buck" McKeon (R-CA) were the Chairman and Ranking Member, respectively, of the House, Armed Services Committee in the 111th Congress. Representative J. Randy Forbes (R-VA) was the other Congressman.

and complete accounting of the analysis supporting the SecDef's recommendation. Congressional leaders of both houses cautioned DoD of the potential for regression in the area of jointness, and the need for someone to maintain a vigilance on jointness.

Despite the controversial nature of the decision to close USJFCOM and the rancor exhibited by Congress over the decision, President Obama's endorsement of the initiative will guarantee the command's closure before the end of 2011. As described in Chapter 5, there are a number of critical functions performed by USJFCOM that must be retained to preserve and promote joint capabilities for the warfighter. Of the six Unified Command Plan (UCP) directed functional responsibilities assigned to USJFCOM, three are specifically recommended to endure: joint force provider, joint force training and exercises, and joint force integration.

Joint Force Provider

Regardless of whether USJFCOM will exist as a separate combatant command, all Services face a crisis in their force planning and procurement plans–force structure is being sacrificed to buy new weapons and recapitalize infrastructure. The DoD faces critical problems in terms of manpower numbers, the balancing of the active and Reserve forces, and deployment cycles[6] that are straining the force. The joint force provider function carried out by USJFCOM, guided by the Global Force Management Implementation Guidance with oversight from the Joint Staff and the SecDef, has served joint warfighters well for nearly two decades. As three of the four Service force managers are located in southeastern Virginia and the joint coordination conducted by USJFCOM has occurred predominantly in that area since 1993, the author's

---

[6] Anthony H. Cordesman, *Reforming Defense Decision-making: Taking Responsibility and Making Meaningful Plans* (Washington, DC: Center For Strategic and International Studies, March 11, 2009).

recommendation is to continue with business as usual and retain responsibility for the coordination in Norfolk, Virginia with oversight by the Joint Staff.

Joint Force Training and Exercises

Insufficient joint training has hindered past American military operations, though not outcomes. With the current drawdown of forces, the inefficiencies of the past caused by insulated, *non-joint* training will be unacceptable in the future. It is imperative that a robust Chairman of the Joint Chiefs of Staff (CJCS) exercise and mission rehearsal exercise program endure to support the training of headquarters units deploying to Afghanistan and Iraq. Further, in order to continue evolving operations, it is necessary to conduct a rigorous operational analysis of current operations. The synthesis or results of the analysis should provide lessons learned which inform best practices. These best practices then must be incorporated and reinforced in joint training and exercises. The author recommends continuing the joint forces training function at the Joint Warfighting Center (JWFC) facility in Suffolk, Virginia. The JWFC has developed and invested in a Joint National Training Center (JNTC) capability that employs joint modeling and simulation tools and technology to simulate varied operational environments. Using a blend of live, virtual and constructive environments, the JNTC provides a venue for training and exercising for current and future conflicts.

Joint Force Integrator

The challenge to joint operations is growing as new technologies are developed and fielded by the Services. While hardware is a Service prerogative, there must be an effort to consider *joint interoperability* at the beginning of each development process. This will ensure that mismatched communications and computers systems do not hamper future operations as was the case during the Operation DESERT STORM or the early phases of Operations IRAQI FREEDOM and ENDURING FREEDOM. Achieving shared situational awareness amongst the joint force mandates compatible information systems and communications architectures. These elements will engender and reinforce the trust and confidence essential to enabling collaborative planning and information sharing–conditions necessary for joint operations.[7] Essential to a successful joint integration program are clear, concise principles and methodologies of joint doctrine. Joint doctrine helps to develop trust by acknowledging Service interdependence and identifying doctrinal concepts, processes and procedures that reduce uncertainty.

With the closure or disestablishment of USJFCOM, the likely overseer of the joint force integration function is the Joint Staff J8. While the Joint Staff J8 is the best place to handle policy, guidance and oversight issues, the author recommends continuing the detailed work of joint force integration responsibilities at the two centers currently performing integration and interoperability testing. The Joint Fires Integration and Interoperability Team (JFIIT) is ideally located at Eglin AFB, Florida to conduct joint assessments and testing to improve the integration, interoperability and effectiveness of joint fires and combat identification at the tactical level. JFIIT develops and improves joint fires solutions that reduce collateral damage and fratricide. The Joint Systems Integration Center (JSIC) facility in Suffolk, Virginia is a state-of-the art system engineering laboratory with the technical expertise to conduct defendable and repeatable scientific methodologies analyzing DoD command and control integration and interoperability issues.

---

[7] National Military Strategy, 17.

Summary

Admiral Mullen, Chairman of the Joint Chiefs of Staff, declared in August 2010, "the single biggest threat to our national security is our debt."[8] The Chairman's admonition about the debt notwithstanding, the haphazard and ill-advised shuttering of USJFCOM also poses a serious threat to our national security. After nearly two decades of operational experience, the Services have demonstrated a high level of competence in the area of jointness. Joint competencies have been achieved principally by two major forcing functions: the necessity of operating jointly against a determined foe in combat, and the promotion of joint matters by USJFCOM, the joint force advocate. The critical functions of USJFCOM's work must endure. Working together on lines of operations such as joint training and exercises, joint force interoperability and integration, and joint force provision USJFCOM has fostered a cooperative spirit of jointness among all participants. For these reasons and others specified in this paper, the closure of USJFCOM must be carefully and thoroughly examined to preclude throwing the baby out with the bath water and to ensure that recommended core functions are retained to enable the joint force to succeed in the future.

---

[8] Michael J. Carden, "National Debt Poses Security Threat, Mullen Says," *American Foreign Press Service*, August 27, 2010. http: www.defense.gove/news/newsarticle.aspx?id=60621 (accessed January 10, 2011).

BIBLIOGRAPHY

Ackerman, Robert K. "Jointness Remains An Elusive Target." *Signal*, May 1, 2004. http://www.afcea.org/signal/articles/templates/SIGNAL_Article_Template.asp?a rticleid=138&zoneid=42 (accessed October 14, 2010).

Agnew, Tracy. "Senate Review: Webb Secures Armed Services Committee Inquiry of JFCOM." *Suffolk News Herald*, August 25, 2010.

Bartel, Bill. "JFCOM Will Shut Down in about 10 Months, Commander Says." *Virginia Pilot (Norfolk)*, January 11, 2011. http://hamptonroads.com/2011/01/jfcom-will-shut-down-about-10-months-commander-says (accessed January 13, 2011).

Boyer, Jacob. "USJFCOM Planners Play Vital Role in Force Deployment." USJFCOM: Ready for Today, Preparing for Tomorrow. http://www.jfcom.mil/newslink/storyarchive/2009/pa120809.html (accessed February 23, 2011).

Brackell, Robert. "Joint Force Provider." The New Atlanticist Policy and Analysis Blog. acus.org/new_atlanticist/joint-force-provider (accessed February 23, 2011).

Brodsky, Robert. "Lawmakers Seek Justification for Closing Joint Forces Command." *Government Executive*, October 15, 2010, Unknown. http://www.govexec.com/story_page.cfm?filepath=/dailyfed/101510rb1.htm&ore f=search (accessed December 23, 2010).

Carden, Michael C. "Defense.gov News Article: National Debt Poses Security Threat, Mullen Says." The Official Home of the Department of Defense. http://www.defense.gov/news/newsarticle.aspx?id=60621 (accessed January 21, 2011).

Casper, Robert. *Dissolving U.S. Joint Forces Command*. Ft. Belvoir, VA: Defense Technical Information Center, 252006.

Chairman of the Joint Chiefs of Staff Instruction (CJCSI) 3100.01B, Joint Strategic Planning System. Washington, DC: Joint Chiefs of Staff, 2008.

Chairman of the Joint Chiefs of Staff Manual (CJCSM) 3500.03B, Joint Training Manual for the Armed Forces of the United States. Washington, DC: Joint Chiefs of Staff, 2008.

Chairman of the Joint Chiefs of Staff. "National Military Strategy of the U.S.-A Strategy for Today; A Vision for Tomorrow." U.S. Department of Defense. www.defense.gov/news/mar2005/d20050318nms.pdf (accessed March 8, 2011).

Cohen, William S. *Defense Reform Initiative Report*. Washington, DC: Office of the

Secretary of Defense, 1997.

Cole, Ronald H. *The History of the Unified Command Plan, 1946-1999*. Washington, DC: Joint History Office, Office of the Chairman of the Joint Chiefs Of Staff, 2003.

Cordesman, Anthony H. *Reforming Defense Decision-making: Taking Responsibility and Making Meaningful Plans*. Washington, DC: Center for Strategic and International Studies Report, 2009.

Debt, Deficits, and Defense: A Way Forward. Washington, DC: Sustainable Defense Task Force, 2010.

Delisle, Elizabeth C., and Barbara Edwards, et al. "Monthly Budget Review Fiscal Year 2010." Monthly Budget Review. www.cbo.gov/ftpdocs/119xx/doc11936/SeptemberMBR.pdf (accessed January 21, 2011).

Department of Defense Dictionary of Military and Associated Terms. Ft. Belvoir, VA: Defense Technical Information Center, 302008.

Doctrine for the Armed Forces of the United States. Washington, DC: Joint Chiefs of Staff, 2009.

Drew, Dennis. "Jointness the Fundamental Problem: A Review of Joint Pub 1." *Airpower Journal* VI, no. 2, (1992): 46-50.

Gates, Robert M. "Statement on Department Budget and Efficiencies." Speech, Secretary of Defense Press Conference from Pentagon, Department of Defense, Arlington, VA, January 6, 2011.

Gates, Robert M. "Statement on Department Efficiencies Initiative." Speech, Secretary of Defense Press Conference from Pentagon, Department of Defense, Arlington, VA, August 9, 2010.

Goldwater-Nichols Department of Defense Reorganization Act of 1986. Public Law 99-433. Washington, DC: U.S. Government Printing Office, October 1, 1986.

Gordon, Michael R., and Bernard E. Trainor. *The Generals' War: The Inside Story of the Conflict in the Gulf*. Boston: Little, Brown, 1995.

Hautau, Charles A. *Joint Training-Future Dilemmas and Solutions*. Ft. Belvoir, VA: Defense Technical Information Center, 181993.

Herrly, Peter F. "Joint Warfare-The American Way of War." *Military Review* 72, no. 2 (1992): 10-15.

Hirrel, Leo P, and William R. McClintock. *United States Joint Forces Command: Sixtieth Anniversary, 1947-2007.* Norfolk, VA: Office of the Command Historian, 2007.

Hirrel, Leo P. *U.S. Joint Forces Command Historical Report, November 2005 to November 2007.* Norfolk, VA: Office of the Command Historian, U.S. Joint Forces Command, 2009.

"HRPDC JFCOM Economic Impact Brief No. 1 Aug 19, 2010." Hampton Roads Planning District Commission. www.hrpdc.org/Documents/Economics/2010/JFCOM_Economic_Impact_Brief. pdf (accessed March 9, 2011).

Killebrew, Bob. "Goodbye JFCOM." *Armed Forces Journal,* 11/2010 (2010). http://www.armedforcesjournal.com/2010/11/4783736/ (accessed February 23, 2011).

Kreisher, Otto. "The Quest for Jointness." *Air Force Magazine* 84, no. 9 (2001): 73-76.

Locher III, James. "Has it Worked? The Goldwater-Nichols Reorganization Act." *Naval War College Review* Volume LIV, no. 4, Autumn 2001 (2001): 95-115.

McKeon, Howard P. "Buck", J. Randy Forbes, and Robert J. Wittman. "HASC Letter to Secretary of Defense." Congressman J. Randy Forbes. forbes.house.gov/UploadedFiles/HPMForbesWittman_to_SecDef_re_Efficiencie s.pdf (accessed December 23, 2010).

Miles, Donna. "DefenseLINK News: 'Jointness' Becomes Key Focus in Developing Military Capability." GlobalSecurity.org - Reliable Security Information. http://www.globalsecurity.org/military/library/news/2006/03/mil-060314-afps02.htm (accessed February 23, 2011).

"Mr. Potato Head." The V&A Museum of Childhood. vam.ac.uk/moc.collections/toys/construction_toys/mr_potato_head (accessed November 3, 2010).

Nemfakos, Charles, and Irv Blickstein, et al. *Perfect Storm: The Goldwater-Nichols Act and its Effect on Navy Acquisition.* Santa Monica, CA: RAND, 2010.

Payne, Kimball. "Virginia Lawmakers Say Joint Forces Closure May be Illegal." *Newport News Daily Press,* August 12, 2010.

Pincus, Walter. "Joint Forces Command, Which Relies on Contractors, Is Tempting Target for Gates." *Washington Post,* August 18, 2010.

Punaro, Arnold. "Reducing Overhead and Improving DoD's Business Operations

Briefing." Defense Business Board. http://dbb.defense.gov/reports2010.shtml (accessed March 9, 2011).

Report of the Tenth Quadrennial Review of Military Compensation. Volumes I & II. Ft. Belvoir, VA: Defense Technical Information Center, 2008.

Roman, Peter J., and David W. Tarr. "The Joint Chiefs of Staff: From Service Parochialism to Jointness." *Political Science Quarterly* 113, no. 1 (1998): 91-111.

Rubel, Robert. "Principles of Jointness." *Joint Forces Quarterly* Winter 2000-01, no. 27 (2000): 45-49.

Scully, Megan. "Webb to Stall Future Defense Nominations over JFCOM." *Government Executive*, October 26, 2010. http://www.govexec.com/story_page.cfm?filepath=/dailyfed/1010/102610nj2.htm&oref=search (accessed December 23, 2010).

Story, William C. *Military Changes to the Unified Command Plan: Background and Issues for Congress.* Washington, DC: Congressional Research Service, Library of Congress, 1999.

Tiron, Roxana. "Webb Lifts Hold Over Nominees." *The Hill.com (Washington)*, November 18, 2010. http://thehill.com/homenews/senate/130019-webb-lifts-holds-over-military-nominees (accessed January 17, 2011).

"Title 10, United States Code. Section 2687 Base Realignments and Closures." GPO Access Home Page. http://www.gpoaccess.gov/uscode/index.html (accessed March 9, 2011).

Tyacke, Lorraine E. *A Study of Joint Transformation at United States Joint Forces Command.* Carlisle Barracks, PA: U.S. Army War College, 2002.

Unified Action Armed Forces (UNAAF). Washington, DC: Joint Chiefs of Staff, 2009.

Unified Command Plan. Washington, DC: Joint Chiefs of Staff, 1999.

Unified Command Plan. Washington, DC: Joint Chiefs of Staff, 2008.

U.S. Congress. House, Committee on Armed Services. *Hearing on Defense Department Efficiency Initiative, full committee hearing on subject of elimination of USJFCOM.* Chairman, Congressman Ike Skelton, 111th Cong. 2nd session, September 29, 2010.

U.S. Congress. House, Committee on Armed Services. *Hearing on National Defense*

Authorization Act for Fiscal Year 2008-full committee hearing on budget request from U.S. European Command and U.S. Joint Forces Command. Author: General Lance Smith, USAF. 110th Cong. 1st sess., March 15, 2007.

U.S. Congress. House, Committee on Armed Services. *Hearing on National Defense Authorization Act for Fiscal Year 2011 Budget European Command, African Command, Joint Forces Command.* Author: General James N. Mattis, USMC. 111th Cong. 1st sess., March 10, 2010.

U.S. Congress. Senate, Committee on Armed Services. *Hearing on Defense Department Efficiency Initiative,* Chairman, Senator Carl Levin, 111th Cong. 2nd session, September 28, 2010.

U.S. Joint Forces Command. "Intelligence Directorate (J2) and Joint Intelligence Operations Center (JIOC) Fact Sheet." USJFCOM: Ready for Today, Preparing for Tomorrow. http://www.jfcom.mil/about/abt_j2.htm (accessed October 22, 2010).

U.S. Joint Forces Command. "Joint Center for Operational Analysis (JCOA) Fact Sheet." USJFCOM: Ready for Today, Preparing for Tomorrow. http://www.jfcom.mil/about/fact_jcoa.htm (accessed October 22, 2010).

U.S. Joint Forces Command. "Joint Communications Support Element (JCSE) Fact Sheet." USJFCOM: Ready for Today, Preparing for Tomorrow. www.jfcom.mil/about/com_jcse.htm (accessed October 22, 2010).

U.S. Joint Forces Command. "Joint Concept Development and Experimentation (JCDE) Directorate (J9) Fact Sheet." USJFCOM: Ready for Today, Preparing for Tomorrow. www.jfcom.mil/abt_j9.htm (accessed November 3, 2010).

U.S. Joint Forces Command. "Joint Deployment Training Center (JDTC) Fact Sheet." USJFCOM: Ready for Today, Preparing for Tomorrow. http://www.jfcom.mil/about/com_jdtc.htm (accessed October 22, 2010).

U.S. Joint Forces Command. "Joint Enabling Capabilities Command (JECC) Fact Sheet." USJFCOM: Ready for Today, Preparing for Tomorrow. http://www.jfcom.mil/about/com_jecc.html (accessed October 22, 2010).

U.S. Joint Forces Command. "Joint Fires Integration and Interoperability Team (JFIIT) Fact Sheet." USJFCOM: Ready for Today, Preparing for Tomorrow. http://www.jfcom.mil/about/com_jfiit.htm (accessed October 22, 2010).

U.S. Joint Forces Command. "Joint Irregular Warfare Center (JIWC) Fact Sheet." USJFCOM: Ready for Today, Preparing for Tomorrow. http://www.jfcom.mil/about/abt_jiwc.html (accessed October 26, 2010).

U.S. Joint Forces Command. "Joint Personnel Recovery Agency (JPRA) Fact Sheet."
    USJFCOM: Ready for Today, Preparing for Tomorrow.
    http://www.jfcom.mil/about/com_jpra.htm (accessed October 22, 2010).

U.S. Joint Forces Command. "Joint Public Affairs Support Element (JPASE)."
    USJFCOM: Ready for Today, Preparing for Tomorrow.
    http://www.jfcom.mil/about/abt_jpase.htm (accessed October 22, 2010).

U.S. Joint Forces Command. "Joint Systems Integration Center (JSIC) Fact Sheet."
    USJFCOM: Ready for Today, Preparing for Tomorrow.
    http://www.jfcom.mil/about/com_jsic.htm (accessed October 22, 2010).

U.S. Joint Forces Command. "Joint Training Directorate and Joint Warfighting Center
    (J7) Fact Sheet." USJFCOM: Ready for Today, Preparing for Tomorrow.
    http://www.jfcom.mil/about/abt_j7.html (accessed November 3, 2010).

U.S. Joint Forces Command. "Joint Unmanned Aircraft Systems-Center of Excellence
    (JUAS-COE) Fact Sheet." USJFCOM: Ready for Today, Preparing for
    Tomorrow. http://www.jfcom.mil/about/com_juas.html (accessed October 26,
    2010).

U.S. Joint Forces Command. "Joint Warfare Analysis Center (JWAC) Fact Sheet."
    USJFCOM: Ready for Today, Preparing for Tomorrow.
    http://www.jfcom.mil/about/com_jwac.htm (accessed October 22, 2010).

U.S. Joint Forces Command. *U.S. Joint Forces Command Overview Briefing.* Norfolk,
    VA: USJFCOM Public Affairs Office, 2010.

U.S. Joint Forces Command. "Special Operations Command JFCOM (SOCJFCOM) Fact
    Sheet. " USJFCOM: Ready for Today, Preparing for Tomorrow.
    http://www.jfcom.mil/about/com_socjfcom.htm (accessed October 26, 2010).

U.S. Joint Forces Command. "USJFCOM: About the Force Provider Mission."
    USJFCOM: Ready for Today, Preparing for Tomorrow.
    http://www.jfcom.mil/about/forceprov.html (accessed March 8, 2011).

U.S. President. *Presidential Memorandum-Disestablishment of United States Joint
    Forces Command.* Washington, DC: Office of the White House Press Secretary,
    2011.

Weitz, Richard. "Jointness and Desert Storm: A Retrospective." *Defense and Security
    Analysis* 20, no. 2 (2004): 133-152.

Wood, John. Interview by Dr. Leo P Hirrel. Personal interview. Norfolk, VA, September
    10, 2008.

Woodward, Bob. *Plan of Attack*. New York: Simon & Schuster, 2004.